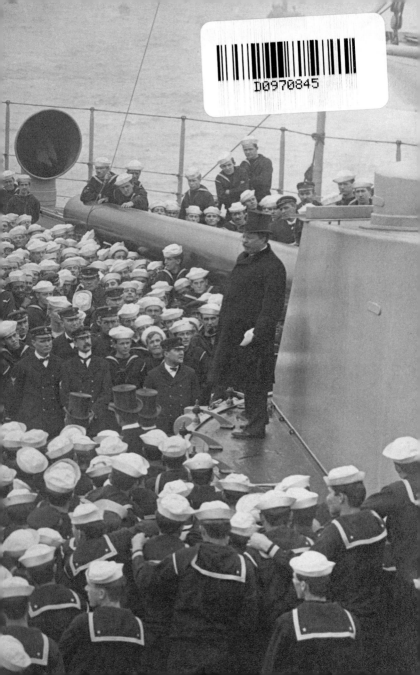

THEODORE ROOSEVELT

HIS ESSENTIAL WISDOM

THEODORE ROOSEVELT

HIS ESSENTIAL WISDOM

EDITED BY CAROL KELLY-GANGI

FALL RIVER PRESS

New York

To John—
Thank you for loving history with me.

FALL RIVER PRESS

New York

An Imprint of Sterling Publishing
387 Park Avenue South
New York, NY 10016

Book and jacket design by Scott Russo

ISBN 978-1-4351-4682-2

Distributed in Canada by Sterling Publishing
c/o Canadian Manda Group, 165 Dufferin Street
Toronto, Ontario, Canada M6K 3H6
Distributed in the United Kingdom by GMC Distribution Services
Castle Place, 166 High Street, Lewes, East Sussex, England BN7 1XU
Distributed in Australia by Capricorn Link (Australia) Pty. Ltd.
P.O. Box 704, Windsor, NSW 2756, Australia

For information about custom editions, special sales, and premium and
corporate purchases, please contact Sterling Special Sales at 800-805-5489
or specialsales@sterlingpublishing.com.

Manufactured in the United States of America

2 4 6 8 10 9 7 5 3 1

www.sterlingpublishing.com

CONTENTS

INTRODUCTION

"THE LIGHT HAS GONE OUT OF MY LIFE."
　　　—Roosevelt's diary entry after his beloved mother and wife died within
　　　hours of each other on February 14, 1884

J ust days before Theodore Roosevelt penned these despondent words, he had been happier than he could have ever imagined. A child born to wealth and privilege, "Teedie" had been raised in a loving home with siblings, extended family, and parents whom he adored. He overcame the effects of acute asthma through vigorous exercise and the sheer strength of will to improve his body to match his facile mind. Harvard-educated, and married to the woman of his dreams, he was already a successful writer, and a fast-rising politician who'd been sworn in as the youngest member of the New York State Legislature less than two years earlier. But with the tragic loss of the two women he loved best in the world, he was shattered. He entrusted his newborn daughter to the care of his sister, Anna, and fled to the West, seemingly done with public life for good.

But Roosevelt's time in the West—spent working and living among ranch hands and experiencing the desolate beauty of the Badlands—

renewed him in mind, body, and spirit, and paved the way for his return to a life of vitality once more. He found love again with his childhood friend Edith Kermit Carow. Their lifetime of devotion to each other and to their brood of children is well documented. His return to public life included stints as the U.S. Civil Service commissioner, police commissioner of New York City, assistant secretary of the navy, colonel in the Spanish-American War, governor of New York, vice president, and, finally, the president of the United States. His presidency was marked by bold leadership and a landslide of landmark reforms that forever changed our nation. Considered by historians as the architect of the modern presidency, Roosevelt was a firm believer in strong executive powers. He deftly wielded the might of the federal government to break the stranglehold of the trusts; improve working conditions for average Americans; provide safe food and drugs; and in perhaps his most enduring legacy, establish sweeping conservation programs to ensure that generations to come would enjoy the rich resources, varied plant and animal life, and rare beauty of the land he loved so much.

Theodore Roosevelt: His Essential Wisdom collects more than three hundred quotations from Roosevelt, culled from his speeches, books, essays, articles, letters, diaries, and other writings. His status as one of the nation's most prolific presidents is evidenced by the massive output of written material in his 60-year lifetime. It is estimated that he penned 150,000 letters and wrote more than twenty books in the fields of history, literature, biography, politics, memoir, and natural history; this is in addition to his many speeches and presidential messages.

Arranged thematically, the excerpts provide a glimpse into the great intellect, strong leadership style, and passionate views that marked Roosevelt's life in public service. In the selections, he vividly expresses his staunch beliefs in America's greatness and the role it was destined to play on the world stage. He speaks passionately about the rule of law, the quest for equality, and the need for justice if America is to fulfill the promise set forth by the Founders. He details the need for reform in key areas of American life in order to provide the "square deal" that every citizen deserves.

Other excerpts reveal a more personal side of this great leader. He reverentially recalls his father, and the driving impetus he felt to live up to the Roosevelt name. Letters and diary entries reveal the depths of despair he felt at the loss of his mother and young wife. In later selections, the love and devotion he felt for Edith and their six children reveal him as a doting and tender husband and father. Still other excerpts shed light on his deeply enriching lifelong romance with the natural world. The last chapter's quotations from friends, family, fellow naturalists, politicians, historians, and writers provide invaluable insights into this electrifying man and remarkable leader.

In a time when political division continues to mar the American landscape, Theodore Roosevelt stands firm as one of America's greatest leaders—not just for the bold innovation of his presidency, but also his courage in the face of adversity, his vast knowledge of the world and America's place in it, and the extraordinary content of his character.

—Carol Kelly-Gangi, 2013

EARLY YEARS

My father, Theodore Roosevelt, was the best man I ever knew. He combined strength and courage with gentleness, tenderness, and great unselfishness. He would not tolerate in us children selfishness or cruelty, idleness, cowardice, or untruthfulness. As we grew older he made us understand that the same standard of clean living was demanded for the boys as for the girls; that what was wrong in a woman could not be right in a man. With great love and patience and the most under-standing sympathy and consideration, he combined insistence on disci-pline. He never physically punished me but once, but he was the only man of whom I was ever really afraid. I do not mean that it was a wrong fear, for he was entirely just, and we children adored him.

—*An Autobiography*, 1913

I was a sickly, delicate boy, suffered much for asthma, and frequently had to be taken away on trips to find a place where I could breathe. One of my memories is of my father walking up and down the room with me in his arms at night when I was a very small person, and of sitting up in bed gasping, with my father and mother trying to help me.

—*An Autobiography*, 1913

My mother, Martha Bulloch, was a sweet, gracious, beautiful Southern woman, a delightful companion and beloved by everybody. She was entirely "unreconstructed" to the day of her death. Her mother, my grandmother, one of the dearest of old ladies, lived with us, and was distinctly overindulgent to us children, being quite unable to harden her heart towards us even when the occasion demanded it.

—*An Autobiography*, 1913

My father worked hard at his business, for he died when he was forty-six, too early to have retired. He was interested in every social reform movement, and he did an immense amount of practical charitable work himself. He was a big, powerful man, with a leonine face, and his heart filled with gentleness for those who needed help or protection, and with the possibility of much wrath against a bully or an oppressor.

—*An Autobiography*, 1913

You have the mind but not the body. You must make your body.

—Admonition to young Theodore from his father, "Thee," quoted in
Lion in the White House: A Life of Theodore Roosevelt by Aida D. Donald

It was this summer [Roosevelt's thirteenth year] that I got my first gun, and it puzzled me to find that my companions seemed to see things to shoot at which I could not see at all. One day they read aloud an advertisement in huge letters on a distant billboard, and I then realized that something was the matter, for not only was I unable to read the sign but I could not even see the letters. I spoke of this to my father, and soon afterwards got my first pair of spectacles, which literally opened an entirely new world to me. I had no idea how beautiful the world was until I got those spectacles. I had been a clumsy and awkward little boy, and while much of my clumsiness and awkwardness was doubtless due to general characteristics, a good deal of it was due to the fact that I could not see and yet was wholly ignorant that I was not seeing.

—*An Autobiography*, 1913

I left college and entered the big world owing more than I can express to the training I had received, especially in my own home; but with much else also to learn if I were to become really fitted to do my part in the work that lay ahead for the generation of Americans to which I belonged.

—*An Autobiography,* 1913

At last everything is settled; but it seems impossible to realize it. I am so happy that I dare not trust in my own happiness. I drove over to the Lees determined to make an end of things at last; it was nearly eight months since I had first proposed to her, and I had been nearly crazy during the past year; and after much pleading my own sweet, pretty darling consented to be my wife. Oh, how bewitchingly pretty she looked! If loving her with my whole heart and soul can make her happy, she shall be happy; a year ago last Thanksgiving I made a vow that win her I would if it were possible; and now that I have done so, the aim of my whole life shall be to make her happy, and to shield her and guard her from every trial; and, oh, how I shall cherish my sweet queen! How she, so pure and sweet and beautiful can think of marrying me I cannot understand, but I praise and thank God it is so.

—Diary entry, January 25, 1880, quoted in
The Rise of Theodore Roosevelt by Edmund Morris

I answered that if this were so it merely meant that the people I knew did not belong to the governing class, and that the other people did—and that I intended to be one of the governing class; and if they proved too hard-bit for me I supposed I would have to quit, but that I certainly would not quit until I had made the effort and found out whether I really was too weak to hold my own in the rough and tumble.

—Response to relatives' criticism of his joining the local
Republican Association in the fall of 1880, quoted in
The Rise of Theodore Roosevelt by Edmund Morris

Too True! Too True! I have become a "political hack." Finding it would not interfere much with my law I accepted the nomination to the assembly, and was elected by 1500 majority, heading the ticket by 600 votes. But don't think I am going to go into politics after this year, for I am not.

—Letter to Charles Washburn,
November 10, 1881

In answer to your questions I would state that, after having passed through Harvard College, I studied for the bar; but going into politics shortly after leaving college, and finding the work in Albany, if conscientiously done, very harassing, I was forced to take up some out-of-doors occupation for the summer, and now have a cattle ranch in Dakotah. I am a Republican, pure, and simple, neither a "half breed" nor a "stalwart"; and certainly no man, nor yet any ring or clique, can do my thinking for me. As you say, I believe in treating all our business interests equitably and alike; in favoring no one interest or set of interests at the expense of others. . . . for in our present anything but ideal condition of public affairs, honesty and common sense are the two prime requisites for a legislator.

—Letter to Jonas Van Duzer, November 20, 1883

Your words of kind sympathy were very welcome to me. . . . I will try to act in public so as to deserve what you have said of me; though I have not lived long, yet the keenness of joy and the bitterness of sorrow are now behind me; but at least I can live so as not to dishonor the memory of the dead whom I so loved.

—Letter about the deaths of his young wife and his mother, who perished within hours of each other the previous week, to Carl Schurz, February 21, 1884

There were all kinds of things I was afraid of at first, ranging from grizzly bears to "mean" horses and gunfighters; but by acting as if I was not afraid I gradually ceased to be afraid.

—An Autobiography, 1913

AMERICA

Like all Americans, I like big things; big parades, big forests and mountains, big wheat fields, railroads—and herds of cattle too; big factories, steamboats and everything else. But we must keep steadily in mind that no people were ever yet benefited by riches if their property corrupted their virtue. It is of more importance that we should show ourselves honest, brave, truthful, and intelligent than that we should own all the railways and grain elevators in the world . . . I am myself at heart as much a westerner as an easterner; I am proud indeed to be considered one of yourselves, and I address you in the rather solemn strain today only because of my pride in you and because your welfare, morale as well as material, is so near my heart.

—Roosevelt's first major public speech,
Dickinson, Dakota Territory, July 4, 1886

We Americans have many grave problems to solve, many threatening evils to fight, and many deeds to do, if, as we hope and believe, we have the wisdom, the strength, and the courage and the virtue to do them. But we must face the facts as they are. We must neither surrender ourselves to foolish optimism, nor succumb to a timid and ignoble pessimism.

—Forum, April 1894

Much has been given us, and much will rightfully be expected from us. We have duties to others and duties to ourselves; and we can shirk neither. We have become a great nation, forced by the fact of its greatness into relations with the other nations of the earth, and we must behave as beseems a people with such responsibilities.

—Inaugural address, March 4, 1905

Our country offers the most wonderful example of democratic government on a giant scale that the world has ever seen; and the peoples of the world are watching to see whether we succeed or fail.

—Speech, Saratoga, New York, September 27, 1910

The first requisite of a good citizen in this republic of ours is that he shall be able and willing to pull his weight.

—Speech, New York City, November 11, 1902

The nation's most valuable asset is the children; for the children are the nation of the future. All people alive to the nation's need should join together to work for the moral, spiritual, and physical welfare of the children in all parts of our land.

—Speech to the National Editorial Association, Jamestown, Virginia, June 10, 1907

There can be no fifty-fifty Americanism in this country. There is room here for only 100 percent Americanism, only for those who are American and nothing else.

—Speech at the Republican Convention, Saratoga, New York, July 18, 1918

There can be no divided allegiance here. Any man who says he is an American but something else also, isn't an American at all. We have room for but one flag, the American flag, . . . We have room for but one language here and that is the English language, for we intend to see that the crucible turns our people out as Americans, of American nationality, and not as dwellers in a polyglot boardinghouse; and we have room for but one soul loyalty, and that loyalty is to the American people.

—Letter to Richard Melancthon Hurd, president of
the American Defense Society, January 3, 1919

The man who loves other countries as much as he does his own is quite noxious a member of society as the man who loves other women as much as he loves his wife.

—"The Monroe Doctrine,"
The Bachelor of Arts, March 1896

To love one's country above all others is in no way incompatible with respecting and wishing well to all others.

—Speech, "The Two Americas," May 20, 1901

Our country has been populated by pioneers, and therefore it has more energy, more enterprise, more expansive power than any other in the wide world.

—Speech at the Minnesota State Fair, September 2, 1901

Every expansion of a great civilized power means a victory for law, order, and righteousness.

—Speech, "Expansion and Peace," December 21, 1899

The nameless pioneers and settlers, the obscure mothers and fathers, the quiet craftsmen and tradesmen; it is only among these that the real story of America is told; it is only among them that the brilliance of liberty may be comprehended.

Is America a weakling, to shrink from the work of the great world powers? No! The young giant of the West stands on a continent and clasps the crest of an ocean in either hand. Our nation, glorious in youth and strength, looks into the future with eager eyes and rejoices as a strong man to run a race.

—Letter to John Hay, American ambassador to the
Court of St. James in London, June 7, 1897

This nation is seated on a continent flanked by two great oceans. It is composed of men the descendants of pioneers, or, in a sense, pioneers themselves; of men winnowed out from among the nations of the Old World by the energy, boldness, and love of adventure found in their own eager hearts. Such a nation, so placed, will surely wrest success from fortune.

—State of the Union Address, December 2, 1902

The men of Yale, the men of the universities, all, who, when the country called, went to give their lives, did more than reflect honor upon the universities from which they came. They did that which they could not have done so well in any other way. They showed that when the time of danger comes, all Americans, whatever their social standing, whatever their creed, whatever the training they have received, no matter from what section of the country they have come, stand together as men, as Americans, and are content to face the same fate and do the same duties because fundamentally they all alike have the common purpose to serve the glorious flag of their common country.

—Speech at the Yale Alumni Dinner,
Brooklyn, New York, March 3, 1899

We must act with justice and broad generosity and charity toward one another and toward all men if we are to make this Republic what it must and shall be made, the nation in all the earth where each man can in best and freest fashion live his own life unwronged by others and proudly careful to wrong no other man.

—Speech, "The Heirs of Abraham Lincoln," Lincoln Day banquet,
New York City, February 12, 1913

It is true of the Nation, as of the individual, that the greatest doer must also be a great dreamer.

—Address, Berkeley, California, 1911

In the last analysis, the most important elements in any man's career must be the sum of those qualities which, in the aggregate, we speak of as character. If he has not got it, then no law that the wit of man can devise, no administration of the law by the boldest and strongest executive, will avail to help him. We must have the right kind of character—character that makes a man, first of all, a good man in the home, a good father, a good husband—that makes a man a good neighbor. You must have that, and, then, in addition, you must have the kind of law and the kind of administration of the law which will give to those qualities in the private citizen the best possible chance for development. The prime problem of our nation is to get the right type of good citizenship, and, to get it, we must have progress, and our public men must be genuinely progressive.

—Speech, "The New Nationalism," Osawatomie, Kansas,
August 31, 1910

POLITICS, POLITICIANS, AND POLITICAL PARTIES

My first days in the legislature were much like those of a boy in a strange school. My fellow legislators and I eyed one another with mutual distrust. . . . My friendships were made, not with regard to party lines, but because I found, and my friends found, that we had the same convictions on questions of principle and questions of policy.

—*An Autobiography*, 1913

In politics, as in life generally, the strife is well-nigh unceasing and breathing spots are few. Even if the struggle results in a victory, it usually only opens the way for another struggle.

—Letter to his son Ted, January 29, 1904

Perhaps the most important thing the ordinary citizen, and, above all, the leader of ordinary citizens, has to remember in political life is that he must not be a sheer doctrinaire. The closet philosopher, the refined and cultured individual who from his library tells how men ought to be governed under ideal conditions, is of no use in actual governmental work; and the one-sided fanatic, and still more the mob-leader, and the insincere man who to achieve power promises what by no possibility can be performed, are not merely useless but noxious.

—Address at the Sorbonne, "Citizenship in a Republic," Paris, April 23, 1910

Honesty and common sense are the two prime requisites for a legislator.

—Speech, Albany, New York, 1883

I have been accused of many things when I was an executive officer, but never of lack of independence. No public servant who is worth his salt should hesitate to stand by his conscience, and if necessary, to surrender his office rather than to yield his conscientious conviction in a case of any importance.

—Address to the Civic Forum and the Child Welfare League,
New York City, October 20, 1911

A man may neglect his political duties because he is too lazy, too selfish, too short-sighted, or too timid; but whatever the reason may be it is certainly an unworthy reason, and it shows either a weakness or worse than a weakness in the man's character.

—Address to Harvard Union, Harvard University,
Cambridge, Massachusetts, February 23, 1907

There are plenty of decent legislators, and plenty of able legislators; but the blamelessness and the fighting edge are not always combined. Both qualities are necessary for the man who is to wage active battle against the powers that prey. He must be clean of life, so that he can laugh when his public or his private record is searched; and yet being clean of life will not avail him if he is either foolish or timid. He must walk warily and fearlessly, and while he should never brawl if he can avoid it, he must be ready to hit hard if the need arises. Let him remember, by the way, that the unforgivable crime is soft hitting. Do not hit at all if it can be avoided; but never hit softly.

—"Political Politics," *The Outlook*, April 26, 1913

I do not see how bribe-taking among legislators can be stopped until the public conscience, which is, even now, gradually awakening, becomes fully awake to the matter. Then it will stop fast enough; for just as soon as politicians realize that the people are in earnest in wanting a thing done, they make haste to do it.

—*An Autobiography*, 1913

The most successful politician is he who says what everybody is thinking most often and in the loudest voice.

—Quoted in *Treasury of Humorous Quotations* edited by Evan Esar

It is a dreadful misfortune for a man to grow to feel that his whole livelihood and whole happiness depend upon his staying in office.

—Annual Message to Congress, December 2, 1906

Political parties exist to secure responsible government and to execute the will of the people. From these great tasks both of the old parties have turned aside. Instead of instruments to promote the general welfare they have become the tools of corrupt interests, which use them impartially to serve their selfish purposes. Behind the ostensible government sits enthroned an invisible government owing no allegiance and acknowledging no responsibility to the people. To destroy this invisible government, to dissolve the unholy alliance between corrupt business and corrupt politics, is the first task of the statesmanship of the day.

—Speech, "The Progressive Covenant with the People," August 1912

The bosses of the Democratic party and the bosses of the Republican party alike have a closer grip than ever before on the party machines in the States and in the Nation. This crooked control of both the old parties by the beneficiaries of political and business privilege renders it hopeless to expect any far-reaching and fundamental service from either.

—"Platform Insincerity," *The Outlook,* July 27, 1912

No people is wholly civilized where a distinction is drawn between stealing an office and stealing a purse.

—Speech in Chicago, June 22, 1912

I do not number party loyalty among my commandments.

—Quoted in *The Courage and Character of Theodore Roosevelt* by George Grant

My hat is in the ring. The fight is on, and I'm stripped to the buff.

—Roosevelt's remark about his bid for the Republican presidential nomination at a press conference in Cleveland, 1912. Quoted in *Safire's New Political Dictionary* by William Safire

GOVERNMENT AND DEMOCRACY

The object of government is the welfare of the people. The material progress and prosperity of a nation are desirable chiefly so far as they lead to the moral and material welfare of all citizens.

—Speech, "The New Nationalism," Osawatomie, Kansas, August 31, 1910

The government ought not to conduct the business of the country; but it ought to regulate it so that it shall be conducted in the interest of the public.

—Speech at Harrisburg, Pennsylvania, October 4, 1906

The government is us; we are the government, you and I.

—Speech in Asheville, North Carolina, September 9, 1902

The noblest of all forms of government is self-government; but it is also the most difficult.

—Annual Message to Congress, December 5, 1905

The welfare of each of us is dependent fundamentally upon the welfare of all of us, and therefore in public life that man is the best representative of each of us who seeks to do good to each by doing good to all; in other words, whose endeavor it is, not to represent any special class and promote merely that class's selfish interests, but to represent all true and honest men of all sections and all classes and to work for their interests by working for our common country.

—Labor Day address at New York State Fair, September 7, 1903

States' rights should be preserved when they mean the people's rights, but not when they mean the people's wrongs; not, for instance, when they are invoked to prevent the abolition of child labor.

—Address, Cambridge, Massachusetts, February 23, 1907

The majority in a democracy has no more right to tyrannize over a minority than, under a different system, the latter would have to oppress the former.

—Quoted in *The Rise of Theodore Roosevelt* by Edmund Morris

There can be no real political democracy unless there is something approaching an economic democracy.

—"Two Noteworthy Books on Democracy," *The Outlook*, November 18, 1914

A great democracy must be progressive or it will soon cease to be a democracy.

—Speech, "The New Nationalism," Osawatomie, Kansas, August 31, 1910

No student of American history needs to be reminded that the Constitution itself is a bundle of compromises.

—"The College Graduate and Public Life," *Atlantic Monthly*, August 1894

We of the great modern democracies must strive unceasingly to make our several countries lands in which a poor man who works hard can live comfortably and honestly, and in which a rich man cannot live dishonestly nor in slothful avoidance of duty; and yet we must judge rich man and poor man alike by a standard which rests on conduct and not on caste, and we must frown with the same stern severity on the mean and vicious envy which hates and would plunder a man because he is well off and on the brutal and selfish arrogance which looks down on and exploits the man with whom life has gone hard.

—Foreword, *An Autobiography*, 1913

It is the people, and not the judges, who are entitled to say what their constitution means, for the constitution is theirs, it belongs to them and not to their servants in office—any other theory is incompatible with the foundation principles of our government. If we, the people, choose to protect tenement-house dwellers in their homes, or women in sweat-shops and factories, or wage-earners in dangerous and unhealthy trades, or if we, the people, choose to define and regulate the conditions of corporate activity, it is for us, and not for our servants, to decide on the course we deem wise to follow.

—Introduction to William L. Ransom's *Majority Rule and the Judiciary*, July 1, 1912

This country will never really demonstrate that it is a democracy in the full reach and range of that conception until we will have had both a Negro and Jewish president of the United States.

—Roosevelt's remark to Felix Frankfurter,
quoted in *Theodore Roosevelt: A Strenuous Life* by Kathleen Dalton

PRESIDENTS AND THE PRESIDENCY

Lincoln to me has always been a living person, an inspiration and a help. I have always felt that if I could do as he would have done were he in my place, I would not be far from right. And at times when I have been troubled by some public question, I have tried to imagine Lincoln in my position and to do as he would have done.

—Quoted in *Talks with T.R.* edited by John J. Leary, Jr.

His unfaltering resolution, his quiet, unyielding courage, his infinite patience and gentleness, and the heights of disinterestedness which he attained whenever the crisis called for putting aside self, together with his far-sighted, hard-headed common sense point him out as just the kind of chief who can do most good in a democratic republic like ours.

—On Abraham Lincoln, letter to George Otto Trevelyan, March 9, 1905

In the Vice Presidency I could do nothing. I am a comparatively young man yet and I like to work. I do not like to be a figurehead.

—Letter to Henry Cabot Lodge, February 2, 1900

I wish in this campaign to do whatever you think wise and advisable— whatever is likely to produce the best results for the republican ticket. I am strong as a bull moose and you can use me to the limit.

—Letter to Mark Hanna, June 27, 1900

The shock, the grief of the country, are bitter in the minds of all who saw the dark days, while the President yet hovered between life and death. At last the light was stilled in the kindly eyes and the breath went from the lips that even in mortal agony uttered no words save of forgiveness to his murderer, of love for his friends, and of unfaltering trust in the will of the Most High. Such a death, crowning the glory of such a life, leaves us with infinite sorrow, but with such pride in what he had accomplished and in his own personal character, that we feel the blow not as struck at him, but as struck at the Nation. We mourn a good and great President who is dead; but while we mourn we are lifted up by the splendid achievements of his life and the grand heroism with which he met his death.

—State of the Union Address, December 3, 1901

Congress does from a third to a half of what I think is the minimum that it ought to do, and I am profoundly grateful that I get as much.

—Letter to Leonard Wood, March 9, 1905

Much has been given us, and much will rightfully be expected from us. We have duties to others and duties to ourselves; and we can shirk neither. We have become a great nation, forced by the fact of its greatness into relations with the other nations of the earth, and we must behave as beseems a people with such responsibilities. Toward all other nations, large and small, our attitude must be one of cordial and sincere friendship. We must show not only in our words, but in our deeds, that we are earnestly desirous of securing their good will by acting toward them in a spirit of just and generous recognition of all their rights. But justice and generosity in a nation, as in an individual, count most when shown not by the weak but by the strong. While ever careful to refrain from wrongdoing others, we must be no less insistent that we are not wronged ourselves. We wish peace, but we wish the peace of justice, the peace of righteousness. We wish it because we think it is right and not because we are afraid. No weak nation that acts manfully and justly should ever have cause to fear us, and no strong power should ever be able to single us out as a subject for insolent aggression.

—Inaugural address, Washington, D.C., March 4, 1905

The most important factor in getting the right spirit in my Administration, next to the insistence upon courage, honesty, and a genuine democracy of desire to serve the plain people, was my insistence upon the theory that the executive power was limited only by specific restrictions and prohibitions appearing in the Constitution or imposed by the Congress under its Constitutional powers.

—An Autobiography, 1913

In midwinter or midsummer, with Congress sitting or absent, the President has always to be ready to devote every waking hour to some anxious, worrying, harassing matter, most difficult to decide, and yet which is imperative to immediately decide.

—Youth's Companion, November 6, 1902

No single great material work which remains to be undertaken on this continent is of such consequence to the American people as the building of a canal across the Isthmus connecting North and South America. Its importance to the nation is by no means limited merely to its material effects upon our business prosperity; and yet with view to these effects alone it would be to the last degree important for us immediately to begin it. While its beneficial effects would perhaps be most marked upon the Pacific Coast and the Gulf and South Atlantic States, it would also greatly benefit other sections. It is emphatically a work which it is for the interest of the entire country to begin and complete as soon as possible; it is one of those great works which only a great nation can undertake with prospects of success, and which when done are not only permanent assets in the nation's material interests, but standing monuments to its constructive ability.

—State of the Union Address, 1901

To my mind this building of the canal through Panama will rank in kind, though not of course in degree, with the Louisiana Purchase and the acquisition of Texas.

—Letter to Samuel White Small, December 29, 1903

If elected, I shall see to it that every man has a square deal, no less and no more.

—Presidential campaign speech, November 4, 1904

I am criticized for interference with Congress. There really is not any answer I can make to this except to say that if I had not interfered we would not have had any rate bill, or any beef-packers' bill, or any pure-food bill, or any consular reform bill, or the Panama Canal, or the Employers' Liability Bill, or in short, any of the legislation which we have obtained during the last year.

—Letter to Jacob Riis, June 26, 1906

I am not a college freshman . . . and therefore I am not concerned about my "popularity" save in exactly so far as it is an instrument which will help me to achieve my purposes.

—Letter to Sereno S. Pratt, March 1, 1906

I believe what I did in settling the anthracite coal strike was a matter of very real moment from the standpoint not only of industrial but of social reform and progress.

—Letter to Sidney Brooks, December 28, 1908

I have been criticized for shifting and changing my cabinet so often, but I do it with a purpose. Just as soon as a Secretary of the Navy or Interior or any other department gets rusty or else settles down to ease and comfort I transfer him so that he will use the energy, which made him valuable in the first place, in some other department which needs bolstering up. I have not hesitated to drop cabinet officers when I found them inefficient, even though my affections for them urged me to retain them. It is so easy to put one's personal affections for men above the public service.

—Quoted in *The Letters of Archie Butt: Personal Aide to President Roosevelt*

The best executive is one who has sense enough to pick good people to do what he wants done, and self-restraint enough to keep from meddling with them while they do it.

I believe in a strong executive; I believe in power; but I believe that responsibility should go with power, and that it is not well that the strong executive should be a perpetual executive. Above all and beyond all I believe as I have said before that the salvation of this country depends upon Washington and Lincoln representing the type of leader to which we are true. I hope that in my acts I have been a good President, a President who has deserved well of the Republic; but most of all, I believe that whatever value my service may have comes even more from what I am than from what I do. I may be mistaken, but it is my belief that the bulk of my country-men, the men whom Abraham Lincoln called "the plain people"— the farmers, mechanics, small tradesmen, hard-working professional men—feel that I am in a peculiar sense their President, that I represent the democracy in somewhat the fashion that Lincoln did, that is, not in any demagogic way but with a sincere effort to stand for a government by the people and for the people.

—Letter to George Otto Trevelyan, June 19, 1908, quoted in
The Selected Letters of Theodore Roosevelt edited by H. W. Brands

I have a very definite philosophy about the Presidency. I think it should be a very powerful office, and I think the President should be a very strong man who uses without hesitation every power that the position yields; but because of this fact I believe that he should be sharply watched by the people [and] held to a strict accountability by them.

—Letter to Henry Cabot Lodge, July 19, 1908

I do not believe there is any danger of . . . an assault upon my life. . . . And if there were, it would be simple nonsense to try to prevent it, for, as Lincoln said, though it would be safer for a President to live in a cage, it would interfere with his business.

—Letter to Henry Cabot Lodge, August 6, 1906

I determined on the move without consulting the Cabinet, precisely as I took Panama without consulting the Cabinet. A council of war never fights, and in a crisis, the duty of a leader is to lead and not to take refuge behind the generally timid wisdom of a multitude of counselors.

—An Autobiography, 1913

The President is merely the most important among a large number of public servants. He should be supported or opposed exactly to the degree which is warranted by his good conduct or bad conduct, his efficiency or inefficiency in rendering loyal, able, and disinterested service to the Nation as a whole. Therefore it is absolutely necessary that there should be full liberty to tell the truth about his acts, and this means that it is exactly necessary to blame him when he does wrong as to praise him when he does right. Any other attitude in an American citizen is both base and servile. To announce that there must be no criticism of the President, or that we are to stand by the President, right or wrong, is not only unpatriotic and servile, but is morally treasonable to the American public. Nothing but the truth should be spoken about him or any one else. But it is even more important to tell the truth, pleasant or unpleasant, about him than about any one else.

—Roosevelt's editorial in the Kansas City Star, May 7, 1918

When I left the Presidency, I finished seven and a half years of administration, during which not one shot had been fired against a foreign foe. We were at absolute peace, and there was no nation in the world whom we had wronged, or from whom we had anything to fear.

—*An Autobiography*, 1913

Power always brings with it responsibility. You cannot have power to work well without having so much power as to be able to work ill.

—Speech, Milwaukee, September 7, 1910

I do not think any two people ever got more enjoyment out of the White House than Mother and I. We love the house itself, without and within, for its associations, for its stillness and its simplicity.

—Letter to his son Ted, May 28, 1904

No other President ever enjoyed the Presidency as I did.

—Letter to George Otto Trevelyan, September 10, 1909

I don't think any President ever enjoyed himself more than I did. Moreover, I don't think any ex-President ever enjoyed himself more.

—Speech at the University of Cambridge, England, May 26, 1910

I do not at all like the social conditions at present. The dull, purblind folly of the very rich men; their greed and arrogance, and the way in which they have unduly prospered by the help of the ablest lawyers, and too often through the weakness or shortsightedness of the judges or by their unfortunate possession of meticulous minds; these facts, and the corruption in business and politics, have tended to produce a very unhealthy condition of excitement and irritation in the popular mind, which shows itself in part in the enormous increase in the socialistic propaganda.

—Letter to future president William H. Taft, 1906

I have enjoyed every moment of this so-called arduous and exacting task.

—Remark to William Jennings Bryan, 1908

It is with peculiar pleasure that I stand here today to express the deep appreciation I feel of the high honor conferred upon me by the presentation of the Nobel Peace Prize. The gold medal which formed part of the prize I shall always keep, and I shall hand it on to my children as a precious heirloom. The sum of money provided as part of the prize by the wise generosity of the illustrious founder of this world-famous prize system, I did not, under the peculiar circumstances of the case, feel at liberty to keep. I think it eminently just and proper that in most cases the recipient of the prize should keep for his own use the prize in its entirety. But in this case, while I did not act officially as President of the United States, it was nevertheless only because I was President that I was enabled to act at all; and I felt that the money must be considered as having been given me in trust for the United States. I therefore used it as a nucleus for a foundation to forward the cause of industrial peace, as being well within the general purpose of your Committee; for in our complex industrial civilization of today the peace of righteousness and justice, the only kind of peace worth having, is at least as necessary in the industrial world as it is among nations. There is at least as much need to curb the cruel greed and arrogance of part of the world of capital, to curb the cruel greed and violence of part of the world of labor, as to check a cruel and unhealthy militarism in international relationships.

—Nobel Peace Prize Acceptance Speech,
Oslo, Norway, May 5, 1910

I wish I were President at this moment! . . . The first thing I would do . . . would be to interfere in the world war on the side of justice and honesty. . . . I do not believe in neutrality between right and wrong. I believe in justice.

—Quoted in *Theodore Roosevelt: The Great Adventure and the Rise of Modern America* by Albert Marrin

EQUALITY, THE LAW, AND JUSTICE

Let the watchwords of all our people be the old familiar watchwords of honesty, decency, fair-dealing, and common sense. . . . We must treat each man on his worth and merits as a man. We must see that each is given a square deal, because he is entitled to no more and should receive no less. The welfare of each of us is dependent fundamentally upon the welfare of all of us.

—Labor Day address at the New York State Fair,
September 7, 1903

There are good men and bad men of all nationalities, creeds, and colors; and if this world of ours is ever to become what we hope some day it may become, it must be by the general recognition that the man's heart and soul, the man's worth and actions, determine his standing.

—Letter to Baron d'Estournelles de Constant, September 1, 1903

I had no thought whatever of anything save of having a chance of showing some little respect to a man whom I cordially esteem as a good citizen and a good American. The outburst of feeling is to me literally inexplicable. It does not anger me. As far as I am personally concerned I regard their attacks with the most contemptuous indifference, but I am very melancholy that such feeling should exist in such bitterly aggravated form.

—Roosevelt's reaction to the outcry against him for inviting Booker T. Washington to
dine at the White House, letter to Lucius Nathan Littauer, October 24, 1901

We can best get justice by doing justice.

—Speech, "National Duties," September 2, 1901

As a people striving to shape our actions in accordance with the great law of righteousness we cannot afford to take part in or be indifferent to the oppression or maltreatment of any man who, against crushing disadvantages, has by his own industry, energy, self-respect, and perseverance struggled upward to a position which would entitle him to the respect of his fellows, if only his skin were of a different hue.

Every generous impulse in us revolts at the thought of a thrusting down instead of helping up such a man. To deny any man the fair treatment granted to others no better than he is to commit a wrong upon him—a wrong sure to react in the long run upon those guilty of such denial. The only safe principle upon which Americans can act is that of "all men up," not that of "some men down."

—Address, "The Negro Problem," Lincoln Dinner of the Republican Club
of the City of New York, February 13, 1905

It was my good fortune at Santiago to serve beside colored troops. A man who is good enough to shed his blood for the country is good enough to be given a square deal afterwards. More than that no man is entitled to, and less than that no man shall have.

—Speech at the Lincoln Monument, Springfield, Illinois, July 4, 1903

We are bound in honor to refuse to listen to those men who would make us desist from the effort to do away with the inequality which means injustice; the inequality of right, opportunity, of privilege. We are bound in honor to strive to bring ever nearer the day when, as far as is humanly possible, we shall be able to realize the ideal that each man shall have an equal opportunity to show the stuff that is in him by the way in which he renders service. There should, so far as possible, be equal of opportunity to render service; but just so long as there is inequality of service there should and must be inequality of reward. . . . But the reward must go to the man who does his work well; for any other course is to create a new kind of privilege, the privilege of folly and weakness; and special privilege is injustice, whatever form it takes.

—Address at the Sorbonne, "Citizenship in a Republic," Paris, April 23, 1910

True liberty shows itself to best advantage in protecting the rights of others, and especially of minorities.

—"Biological Analogies in History," *The Outlook*, June 11, 1910

Viewed purely in the abstract, I think there can be no question that women should have equal rights with men. . . . Especially as regards the laws relating to marriage there should be the most absolute equality between the two sexes. I do not think the woman should assume the man's name.

—Roosevelt's Senior Thesis at Harvard, "The Practicability of Equalizing Men and Women before the Law," 1880

Working women have the same need to protection that working men have; the ballot is as necessary for one class as to the other; we do not believe that with the two sexes there is identity of function; but we do believe there should be equality of right.

—Speech at the National Convention of the Progressive Party, Chicago, August 6, 1912

Much can be done by law towards putting women on a footing of complete and entire equal rights with man—including the right to vote, the right to hold and use property, and the right to enter any profession she desires on the same terms as the man. . . . Women should have free access to every field of labor which they care to enter, and when their work is as valuable as that of a man it should be paid as highly.

—*An Autobiography,* 1913

Brutality by a man to a woman, by a grown person to a little child, by anything strong toward anything good and helpless, makes my blood literally boil. But I hate most of all the crime of a man against a woman. Only less do I hate brutal indifference, the failure to estimate the debt due to the woman who has had a child, and must have in her a touch of a saint—that is, of course, if she has the right spirit in her at all.

—Letter to Hamlin Garland, July 19, 1903

No man is above the law and no man is below it; nor do we ask any man's permission when we require him to obey it. Obedience to the law is demanded as a right; not asked as a favor.

—Annual Message to Congress, December 7, 1903

This country has nothing to fear from the crooked man who fails. We put him in jail. It is the crooked man who succeeds who is a threat to this country.

—Remarks in Memphis, Tennessee, October 25, 1905

The first essential of civilization is law. Anarchy is simply the handmaiden and forerunner of tyranny and despotism. Law and order enforced with justice and by strength lie at the foundations of civilization. Law must be based upon justice, else it cannot stand, and it must be enforced with resolute firmness, because weakness in enforcing it means in the end that there is no justice and no law, nothing but the rule of disorderly and unscrupulous strength. Without the habit of orderly obedience to the law, without the stern enforcement of the laws at the expense of those who defiantly resist them, there can be no possible progress, moral or material, in civilization. There can be no weakening of the law-abiding spirit here at home, if we are permanently to succeed; and just as little can we afford to show weakness abroad.

—Address at the Minnesota State Fair, September 2, 1901

All thoughtful men must feel the gravest alarm over the growth of lynching in this country, and especially over the peculiarly hideous forms so often taken by mob violence when colored men are the victims—on which occasions the mob seems to lay most weight, not on the crime but on the color of the criminal. . . . It is of course inevitable that where vengeance is taken by a mob it should frequently light on innocent people; and the wrong done in such a case to the individual is one for which there is no remedy. But even where the real criminal is reached, the wrong done by the mob to the community itself is well-nigh as great. . . . Whoever in any part of our country has ever taken part in lawlessly putting to death a criminal by the dreadful torture of fire must forever after have the awful spectacle of his own handiwork seared into his brain and soul. He can never be the same man.

—Excerpt from Roosevelt's widely publicized letter to Governor Winfield T. Durbin of Indiana, August 6, 1903

I am glad to see wrong-doers punished, the punishment is an absolute necessity from the standpoint of society; and I put the reformation of the criminal second to the welfare of society. But I do desire to see the man or woman who has paid the penalty and who wishes to reform giving a helping hand—surely every one of us who knows his own heart must know that he too may stumble, and should be anxious to help his brother or sister who has stumbled. When the criminal has been punished, if he then shows a sincere desire to lead a decent and upright life, he should be given the chance, he should be helped and not hindered; and if he makes good, he should receive that respect from others which so often aids in creating self-respect—the most valuable of all possessions.

—*An Autobiography*, 1913

I abhor injustice and bullying by the strong at the expense of the weak.

—*An Autobiography*, 1913

RELIGION, MORALITY, AND VIRTUE

To be just with all men, to be merciful to those to whom mercy should be shown, to realize that there are some things that must always remain a mystery to us, and when the time comes for us to enter the great blackness, to go smiling and unafraid. That is my religion, my faith. To me it sums up all religion, it is all the creed I need. It seems simple and easy, but there is more in that verse than in the involved rituals and confessions of faith of many creeds we know.

—Quoted in *Talks with T.R.* edited by John J. Leary, Jr.

In business and in work, if you let Christianity stop as you go out of the church door, there is little righteousness in you. You must behave to your fellowmen as you would have them behave to you. You must have pride in your work if you would succeed. A man should get justice for himself, but he should also do justice to others. Help a man to help himself, but do not expend all your efforts in helping a man who will not help himself.

—Address at Trinity Reformed Church, Chicago, September 1901

You ask that Mr. Taft shall "let the world know what his religious belief is." This is purely his own private concern; it is a matter between him and his Maker, a matter for his own conscience; and to require it to be made public under penalty of political discrimination is to negative the first principles of our Government, which guarantee complete religious liberty, and the right to each to act in religious affairs as his own conscience dictates. . . . The demand for a statement of a candidate's religious belief can have no meaning except that there may be discrimination for or against him because of that belief. Discrimination against the holder of one faith means retaliatory discrimination against men of other faiths. The inevitable result of entering upon such a practice would be an abandonment of our real freedom of conscience and a reversion to the dreadful conditions of religious dissension which in so many lands have proved fatal to true liberty, to true religion, and to all advance in civilization.

—Letter to J.C. Martin, November 6, 1908

I enter a most earnest plea that in our hurried and rather bustling life of today we do not lose the hold that our forefathers had on the Bible. I wish to see Bible study as much a matter of course in the secular college as in the seminary. . . . I ask that the Bible be studied for the sake of the breadth it must give to every man who studies it.

—Address at the Pacific Theological Seminary, 1911

On Sunday, go to church. Yes, I know all the excuses. I know that one can worship the Creator and dedicate oneself to good living in a grove of trees, or by a running brook, or in one's own house, just as well as in church. But I also know as a matter of cold fact the average man does not thus worship or thus dedicate himself. If he strays away from church, he does not spend his time in good works or lofty meditation. He looks over the colored supplement of the newspaper.

—Quoted in *Ladies Home Journal*, October 1913

Bodily vigor is good, and vigor of intellect is even better, but far above both is character. It is true, of course, that a genius may, on certain lines, do more than a brave and manly fellow who is not a genius; and so, in sports, vast physical strength may overcome weakness, even though the puny body may have in it the heart of a lion. But, in the long run, in the great battle of life, no brilliancy of intellect, no perfection of bodily development, will count when weighed in the balance against that assemblage of virtues, active and passive, of moral qualities, which we group together under the name of character; and if between any two contestants, even in college sport or in college work, the difference in character on the right side is as great as the difference of intellect or strength the other way, it is the character side that will win.

— "Character and Success," *The Outlook*, March 31, 1900

We must all strive to keep as our most precious heritage the liberty each to worship his God as to him seems best, and, as part of this liberty, freely either to exercise it or to surrender it, in a greater or less degree, each according to his own beliefs and convictions, without infringing on the beliefs and convictions of others.

— "The Search for Truth in a Reverent Spirit,"
The Outlook, December 2, 1911

There is always a tendency among very young men and among boys who are not quite young men as yet to think that to be wicked is rather smart; to think it shows that they are men. Oh, how often you see some young fellow who boasts that he is going to "see life," meaning by that that he is going to see that part of life which it is a thousandfold better should remain unseen! I ask that every man here constitute himself his brother's keeper by setting an example to that younger brother which will prevent him from getting such a false estimate of life. Example is the most potent of all things. If any one of you in the presence of younger boys, and especially the younger people of our own family, misbehave yourself, if you use coarse and blasphemous language before them, you can be sure that these younger people will follow your example and not your precept. It is no use to preach to them if you do not act decently yourself. You must feel that the most effective way in which you can preach is by your practice.

—Address, Holy Name Society, Oyster Bay, New York,
August 16, 1903

And character is far more important than intellect in making a man a good citizen or successful at his calling—meaning by character not only such qualities as honesty and truthfulness, but courage, persever-ance, and self-reliance.

— "Professionalism in Sports," *North American Review*, August 1890

If a man does not have an ideal and try to live up to it, then he becomes a mean, base, and sordid creature, no matter how successful. If, on the other hand, he does not work practically, with the knowledge that he is in the world of actual men and must get results, he becomes a worthless head-in-the-air creature, a nuisance to himself and to everybody else.

—Letter to his son Kermit, January 27, 1915

If a man stumbles, it is a good thing to help him to his feet. Every one of us needs a helping hand now and then. But if a man lies down, it is a waste of time to try to carry him; and it is a very bad thing for every one if we make men feel that the same reward will come to those who shirk their work and to those who do it.

—Address at the Sorbonne, "Citizenship in a Republic," Paris, April 23, 1910

I feel very strongly that if any people are oppressed anywhere, the wrong inevitably reacts in the end on those who oppress them; for it is an immutable law in the spiritual world that no one can wrong others and yet in the end himself escape unhurt.

—Letter to Jacob H. Schiff, Chairman,
Committee on the Celebration of the 250th Anniversary of the
Settlement of Jews in the United States, November 16, 1905

From the greatest to the smallest, happiness and usefulness are largely found in the same soul, and the joy of life is won in its deepest and truest sense only by those who have not shirked life's burdens.

—Labor Day address at the New York State Fair, September 7, 1903

PEACE, WAR, THE MILITARY, AND FOREIGN POLICY

We sincerely and earnestly believe in peace; but if peace and justice conflict, we scorn the man who would not stand for justice though the whole world came in arms against him.

—Address at the Sorbonne, "Citizenship in a Republic," Paris, April 23, 1910

Peace is normally a great good, and normally it coincides with righteousness, but it is righteousness and not peace which should bind the conscience of a nation as it should bind the conscience of an individual; and neither a nation nor an individual can surrender conscience to another's keeping.

—Annual Message to Congress, December 4, 1906

It may be that at some time in the dim future of the race the need for war will vanish; but that time is yet ages distant. As yet no nation can hold its place in the world, or can do any work really worth doing, unless it stands ready to guard its rights with an armed hand.

—Speech at Naval War College, Newport, Rhode Island, June 1897

A just war is in the long run far better for a nation's soul than the most prosperous peace obtained by acquiescence in wrong or injustice.

—Annual Message to Congress, December 4, 1906

Colonel Roosevelt, accompanied only by four or five men, led a very desperate and extremely gallant charge on San Juan Hill, thereby setting a splendid example to the troops and encouraging them to pass over the open country intervening between their position and the trenches of the enemy. . . . The charge in itself was an extremely gallant one, and the example set a most inspiring one to the troops in that part of the line. . . . There was no doubt that the magnificent example set by Colonel Roosevelt had a very encouraging effect and had great weight in bringing up the troops behind him. During the assault, Colonel Roosevelt was the first to reach the trenches in his part of the line and killed one of the enemy with his own hand. . . . His services on the day in question were of great value and of a most distinguished character.

—Letter from Major General Leonard Wood to adjutant-general of the army in support of Roosevelt's receiving the Medal of Honor, December 1898. Quoted in *Lion in the White House: A Life of Theodore Roosevelt* by Aida D. Donald

———

No man is worth his salt who is not ready at all times to risk his body, to risk his well-being, to risk his life, in a great cause.

Germany has reduced savagery to a science, and this great war for the victorious peace of justice must go on until the German cancer is cut clean out of the world body.

—Speech in Johnstown, Pennsylvania, September 30, 1917

———

There should be no halt in the work of building up the Navy, providing every year additional fighting craft. We are a very rich country, vast in extent of territory and great in population; a country, moreover, which has an Army diminutive indeed when compared with that of any other first-class power. We have deliberately made our own certain foreign policies which demand the possession of a first-class Navy. The isthmian canal will greatly increase the efficiency of our Navy if the Navy is of sufficient size; but if we have an inadequate Navy, then the building of the canal would be merely giving a hostage to any power of superior strength. The Monroe Doctrine should be treated as the cardinal feature of American foreign policy; but it would be worse than idle to assert it unless we intended to back it up, and it can be backed up only by a thoroughly good Navy. A good Navy is not a provocative of war. It is the surest guaranty of peace.

—State of the Union Address, December 2, 1902

Nothing better for the Navy from every standpoint has ever occurred than the cruise of the battle fleet around the world. The improvement of the ships in every way has been extraordinary, and they have gained far more experience in battle tactics than they would have gained if they had stayed in the Atlantic waters. The American people have cause for profound gratification, both in view of the excellent condition of the fleet as shown by this cruise, and in view of the improvement the cruise has worked in this already high condition.

—State of the Union Address, December 8, 1908

I do not believe in a large standing army. Most emphatically I do not believe in militarism. Most emphatically I do not believe in any policy of aggression by us. But I do believe that no man is really fit to be the free citizen of a free republic unless he is able to bear arms and at deed to serve with efficiency in the efficient army of the republic.

—The New York Times, November 15, 1914

Intelligent foresight in preparation and known capacity to stand well in battle are the surest safeguards against war.

—Roosevelt's preface to Hero Tales, written with Henry Cabot Lodge, 1895

Every man who has in him any real power of joy in battle knows that he feels it when the wolf begins to rise in his heart; he does not then shrink from blood or sweat or deem that they mar the fight; he revels in them, in the toil, the pain, and the danger, as but setting off the triumph.

—"A Colonial Survival," *The Cosmopolitan*, 1893

I am entitled to the Medal of Honor, and I want it.

—Letter to Henry Cabot Lodge, December 1, 1898.
On January 16, 2001, Roosevelt was finally awarded the
Medal of Honor, becoming the first U.S. president to receive it.

Let us speak courteously, deal fairly, and keep ourselves armed and ready.

—Speech, San Francisco, May 13, 1903

I abhor war. In common with all other thinking men I am inexpressibly saddened by the dreadful contest now raging in Europe. I put peace very high as an agent for bringing about righteousness. But if I must choose between righteousness and peace, I choose righteousness.

—*America and the World War*, 1915

Our army needs complete reorganization—not merely enlarging—and the reorganization can only come as the result of legislation. . . . If, during the years to come, any disaster should befall our arms, afloat or ashore, and thereby any shame come to the United States, remember that the blame will lie upon the men whose names appear upon the roll-calls of Congress on the wrong side of these great questions. On them will lie the burden of any loss of our soldiers and sailors, of any dishonor to the flag; and upon you and the people of this country will lie the blame if you do not repudiate, in no unmistakable way, what these men have done.

—Speech, "The Strenuous Life," Chicago, April 10, 1899

A pacifist is as surely a traitor to his country and to humanity as is the most brutal wrongdoer.

—Speech, Pittsburgh, July 27, 1917

I suppose the United States will always be unready for war, and in consequence will always be exposed to great expense, and to the possibility of the gravest calamity, when the nation goes to war. This is no new thing. Americans learn only from catastrophes and not from experience.

—An Autobiography, 1913

The United States ought not to permit any great military powers, which have no foothold on this continent, to establish such foothold; nor should they permit any aggrandizement of those who already have possessions on the continent.

—"The Monroe Doctrine," The Bachelor of Arts, March 1896

More and more the increasing interdependence and complexity of international political and economic relations render it incumbent on all civilized and orderly powers to insist on the proper policing of the world.

—Address to Congress, 1902

Any country whose people conduct themselves well can count upon our hearty friendship. If a nation shows that it knows how to act with reasonable efficiency and decency in social and political matters, if it keeps order and pays its obligations, it need fear no interference from the United States. Chronic wrongdoing, or an impotence which results in a general loosening of the ties of civilized society, may in America, as elsewhere, ultimately require intervention by some civilized nation, and in the Western Hemisphere the adherence of the United States to the Monroe Doctrine may force the United States, however reluctantly, in flagrant cases of such wrongdoing or impotence, to the exercise of an international police power.

—State of the Union Address, December 6, 1904

It is essential that we should have it clearly understood, by our own people especially, but also by other peoples, that the Pacific was as much our home waters as the Atlantic.

—On his sending a U.S. Navy fleet around the world,
An Autobiography, 1913

In my own judgment the most important service that I rendered to peace was the voyage of the battle fleet round the world.

—*An Autobiography*, 1913

I want to make it evident to every foreign nation that I intend to do justice; and neither to wrong them nor to hurt their self-respect; but that on the other, I am both entirely ready and entirely able to see that our rights are maintained in their turn.

—Letter to Whitelaw Reid, December 4, 1908

BUSINESS, LABOR, AND REFORM

We demand that big business give people a square deal; in return we must insist that when any one engaged in big business honestly endeavors to do right, he shall himself be given a square deal.

—About the Taft administration's attempts to dissolve the Steel Trust,
An Autobiography, 1913

Where a trust becomes a monopoly the state has an immediate right to interfere. Care should be taken not to stifle enterprise or disclose any facts of a business that are essentially private; but the State for the protection of the public should exercise the right to inspect, to examine thoroughly all the workings of great corporations just as is now done with banks; and wherever the interests of the public demand it, it should publish the results of its examination.

—Message to the New York State Legislature by Governor Roosevelt,
Albany, New York, January 3, 1900

I believe that monopolies, unjust discriminations, which prevent or cripple competition, fraudulent overcapitalization, and other evils in trust organizations and practices which injuriously affect interstate trade can be prevented under the power of the Congress to "regulate commerce with foreign nations and among the several States" through regulations and requirements operating directly upon such commerce, the instrumentalities thereof, and those engaged therein.

—State of the Union Address, December 2, 1902

The first essential in determining how to deal with the great industrial combinations is knowledge of the facts—publicity. In the interest of the public, the Government should have the right to inspect and examine the workings of the great corporations engaged in interstate business. Publicity is the only sure remedy which we can now invoke. What further remedies are needed in the way of governmental regulation, or taxation, can only be determined after publicity has been obtained, by process of law, and in the course of administration. The first requisite is knowledge, full and complete—knowledge which may be made public to the world.

—State of the Union Address, December 3, 1901

I believe in property rights; I believe that normally the rights of property and humanity coincide; but sometimes they conflict, and where this is so, I put human rights above property rights.

—"Democratic Ideals," *The Outlook*, November 15, 1913

I believe in labor unions. If I were a wageworker I should certainly join one; and I am now an honorary member of one and am very proud of it. But if the members of labor unions indulge in rioting and violence, or behave wrongfully either to a capitalist or to another laborer or to the general public, I shall antagonize them just as fearlessly as under similar circumstances I should antagonize the biggest capitalist in the land.

—Letter to Ray Stannard Baker, August 27, 1904

Our aim is not to do away with corporations; on the contrary, these big aggregations are an inevitable development of modern industrialism, and the effort to destroy them would be futile unless accomplished in ways that would work the utmost mischief to the entire body politic. We can do nothing of good in the way of regulating and supervising these corporations until we fix clearly in our minds that we are not attacking the corporations, but endeavoring to do away with any evil in them. We are not hostile to them; we are merely determined that they shall be so handled as to subserve the public good. We draw the line against misconduct, not against wealth.

—State of the Union Address, December 2, 1902

I believe in corporations. If a corporation is doing square work I will help it so far as I can. If it oppresses anybody; if it is acting dishonestly towards its stockholders or the public, or towards its laborers, or towards small competitors—why, when I have power I shall try to cinch it.

—Letter to Ray Stannard Baker, August 27, 1904

The corporation or individual capitalist paying a starvation wage to an employee, and especially to a woman employee, is guilty of iniquity, and is an enemy of morality, of religion and of the state. Let us as a people face the fact that there must be a living wage for every employee; and that the employer who does not give it is a bad citizen.

—"Cause of Decency," The Outlook, July 15, 1911

The people of the United States have but one instrument which they can efficiently use against the colossal combination of business—and that instrument is the government of the United States.

—Address at the Coliseum, San Francisco, September 14, 1912

It is essential that there should be organizations of labor. This is an era of organization. Capital organizes and therefore labor must organize.

—Speech in Milwaukee, October 14, 1912

The man who wrongly holds that every human right is secondary to his profit must now give way to the advocate of human welfare, who rightly maintains that every man holds his property subject to the general right of the community to regulate its use to whatever degree the public welfare may require it.

—Speech, "The New Nationalism," Osawatomie, Kansas, August 31, 1910

He who counsels violence does the cause of labor the poorest service. Also, he loses the case.

—Remarks by New York City Police Commissioner
Roosevelt to striking workers, 1895

It is contemptible to oppose a movement for good because that movement has already succeeded somewhere else, or to champion an existing abuse because our people have always been wedded to it. To appeal to national prejudice against a given reform movement is in every way unworthy and silly.

—"True Americanism," *The Forum*, April 1894

I have two concerns . . . I hope to see such laws enacted as will prevent the administration of immigrants who by their competition tend to lower the standard of living, and therefore the standard of wages of our own laboring men. . . . But in the next and more important place, it seems to me essential from the standpoint of the permanent good of the Republic that we should try only to bring in elements which would be [of] advantage to our community. I do not care what the man's creed or nationality may be, so long as his character is all right and so long as he has the amount of physical and mental fitness that we should be able to demand.

—Letter to Speaker Cannon, quoted in *Lion in the White House:
A Life of Theodore Roosevelt* by Aida D. Donald. Roosevelt's
efforts to reform immigration came to fruition with the
passage of the Naturalization Act of 1906.

The purpose of the Civil Service Commission is to secure an absolutely non-partisan public service; to have men appointed to and retained in office wholly without reference to their politics. In other words, we desire to make a man's honesty and capacity to do the work to which he is assigned the sole tests of his appointment and retention.

—*An Autobiography*, 1913

The men with the muck-rakes are often indispensable to the well-being of society; but only if they know when to stop raking the muck.

—Address, "The Man with the Muck-Rake,"
Washington, D.C., April 14, 1906

The citizen must have high ideals, and yet he must be able to achieve them in practical fashion. No permanent good comes from aspirations so lofty that they have grown fantastic and have become impossible and indeed undesirable to realize. The impractical visionary is far less often the guide and precursor than he is the embittered foe of the real reformer, of the man who, with stumblings and shortcomings, yet does in some shape, in practical fashion, give effect to the hopes and desires of those who strive for better things. Woe to the empty phrasemaker, to the empty idealist, who, instead of making ready the ground for the man of action, turns against him when he appears and hampers him when he does work!

—Address at the Sorbonne, "Citizenship in a Republic," Paris, April 23, 1910

As regards children, it is as essential to look after their physical as their mental training. We cannot afford to let children grow up ignorant; and if they are sent to school they cannot, while young, also work hard outside without detriment, physical, mental, and moral. There is urgent need for the health authorities to increase their care over the hygienic conditions and surroundings of children of tender years, and especially to supervise those in the schools. It is a good thing to try to reform bad children, to try to build up degenerate children; but it is an even better thing to try to keep healthy in soul, body, and mind those children who are now sound, but who may easily grow up unsound if no care is taken of them.

—Address at Jamestown Exposition, Virginia, June 10, 1907

Our present system, or rather no system, works dreadful wrong, and is of benefit to only one class of people—the lawyers. When a workman is injured what he needs is not an expensive and doubtful lawsuit, but the certainty of relief through immediate administrative action. The number of accidents which result in the death or crippling of wage-workers, in the Union at large, is simply appalling; in a very few years it runs up a total far in excess of the aggregate of the dead and wounded in any modern war.

—State of the Union Address, December 8, 1908

The policies for which I stand have come to stay. Not only will I not change them, but in their essence they will not be changed by any man that comes after me, unless the reactionaries should have their way. . . . I am amused by the shortsighted folly of the very wealthy men and . . . how large a proportion of them stand for what is fundamentally corrupt and dishonest. Every year I have lived has made me a firmer believer in the plain people—in the men who gave Abraham Lincoln his strength—and has made me feel the distrust of the over educated dilettante type and, above all of . . . the plutocratic type.

—Letter, c. 1907, Quoted in *Lion in the White House: A Life of Theodore Roosevelt* by Aida D. Donald

When laws like workmen's compensation laws and the like are passed, it must always be kept in mind by the legislature that the purpose is to distribute over the whole community a burden that should not be borne only by those least able to bear it—that is, by the injured man or the widow and orphans of the dead man.

—*An Autobiography*, 1913

FAMILY, FRIENDS, AND HOME

I never knew any one who got greater joy out of living than did my father or anyone who more whole-heartedly performed every duty; and no one whom I have ever met approached his combination of enjoyment of life and performance of duty. He and my mother were given to a hospitality that at that time was associated more commonly with southern than northern households; and especially in their later years when they had moved up town, in the neighborhood of Central Park, they kept a charming, open house.

—*An Autobiography*, 1913

I do not think there is a fellow in College who has a family that love him as much as you all do me, and I am sure that there is no one who has a Father who is also his best and most intimate friend, as you are mine. . . . I shall do my best to deserve your trust.

—Letter to Theodore Roosevelt, Sr., October 22, 1876

I feel that if it were not for the certainty, that as he himself has so often said, "he is not dead but gone before," I should almost perish.

—Diary entry following the death of Theodore Roosevelt, Sr., 1878, quoted in *The Rise of Theodore Roosevelt* by Edmund Morris

Back again in my own lovely little home, with the sweetest and prettiest of all little wives—my own sunny darling. I can imagine nothing more happy in life than an evening spent in my cosy little sitting room, before a bright fire of soft coal, my books all around me, and playing backgammon with my own dainty mistress.

—Diary entry, fall 1882, quoted in *The Rise of Theodore Roosevelt* by Edmund Morris

The light has gone out of my life.

—Diary entry on the day that his wife, Alice, and his mother died
within hours of each other, February 14, 1884

She was beautiful in face and form, and lovelier still in spirit; as a flower she grew, and as a fair young flower she died. . . . Fair, pure and joyous as a maiden; loving, tender, and happy as a young wife; when she had just become a mother, when her life seemed to be but just begun, and when the years seemed so bright before her—then, by a strange and terrible fate, death came to her. . . . And when my heart's dearest died, the light went out of my life forever.

—Diary entry after the death of Alice Lee Roosevelt, February 1884, quoted
in *The Roosevelts: An American Saga* by Peter Collier with David Horowitz

---

I shall be very, very glad to see you all again. I hope Mousiekins will be very cunning; I shall dearly love her. I suppose all of our friends the unco' good are as angry as ever with me; they had best not express their discontent to my face unless they wish to hear very plain English. I am sorry my political career should be over, but after all it makes very little difference.

—Letter to his sister Anna Roosevelt, September 20, 1884.
After Alice's death, Roosevelt entrusted his sister with his baby
daughter's care, while he fled to the West to escape his grief

---

I have written Nannie telling her that on Saturday next I sail for England to marry Edith Carow. The chief reason I was so especially disappointed at not seeing you both this fall was because I wished to tell you in person. You know, old fellow, you and Nannie are more to me than any one else but my own immediate family. The engagement is not to be announced, nor a soul told, until the 8th.

—Letter to Henry Cabot Lodge, November 1, 1886

A man must be a good son, husband and father, a woman a good daughter, wife and mother, first and foremost.

—Speech, New York City, December 30, 1900

Alone of human beings the good and wise mother stands on a plane of equal honor with the bravest soldier; for she has gladly gone down to the brink of the chasm of darkness to bring back the children in whose hands rests the future.

—The Great Adventure, 1918

The welfare of the woman is even more important than the welfare of the man; for the mother is the real Atlas, who bears aloft in her strong and tender arms the destiny of the world.

—"Rural Life," The Outlook, August 27, 1910

At Sagamore Hill we love a great many things—birds and trees and books, and all things beautiful, and horses and rifles and children and hard work and the joy of life. We have great fireplaces, and in them the logs roar and crackle during the long winter evenings. The big piazza is for the hot, still afternoons of summer.

—An Autobiography, 1913

There is nothing in the world—no possible success, military or political which is worth weighing in the balance for one moment against the happiness that comes to those fortunate enough to make a real love match—a match in which lover and sweetheart will never be lost in husband and wife. . . . I am just as much devoted to Mrs. Roosevelt now as ever I was.

—About his wife, Edith, circa 1900, quoted in *Lion in the White House: A Life of Theodore Roosevelt* by Aida D. Donald

For unflagging interest and enjoyment, a household of children, if things go reasonably well, certainly makes all other forms of success and achievement lose their importance by comparison.

—*An Autobiography*, 1913

When I started for my regiment, in '98, the stress of leaving home, which was naturally not pleasant, was somewhat lightened by the next to the youngest boy, whose ideas of what was about to happen were hazy, clasping me round the legs with a beaming smile and saying, "And is my father going to the war? And will he bring me back a bear?" When, some five months later, I returned, of course in my uniform, this little boy was much puzzled as to my identity, although he greeted me affably with "Good afternoon, Colonel." Half an hour later somebody asked him, "Where's father?" to which he responded, "I don't know; but the Colonel is taking a bath."

—*An Autobiography*, 1913

If however you wish to keep her write her letters—interesting letters, and love letters—at least three times a week. Write no matter how tired you are, no matter how inconvenient it is; write if you're smashed up in a hospital; write when you are doing your most dangerous stunts; write when your work is most irksome and disheartening; write all the time! Write enough letters to allow for half being lost.

—Letter to Quentin, about how to hold on to his sweetheart, Flora, during the war, December 24, 1917, quoted in *The Selected Letters of Theodore Roosevelt* edited by H.W. Brands

I miss you all dreadfully, and the house feels big and lonely and full of echoes with nobody but me in it; and I do not hear any small scamps running up and down the hall just as hard as they can; or hear their voices while I am dressing; or suddenly look out through the windows of the office at the tennis ground and see them racing over it or playing in the sand-box. I love you very much.

—Letter to his son Quentin, written from the White House on April 1, 1906, quoted in *A Bully Father: Theodore Roosevelt's Letters to His Children* by Joan Paterson Kerr

I would rather have a boy of mine stand high in his studies than high in athletics, but I would a good deal rather have him show true manliness of character than show either intellectual or physical prowess.

—Letter to his son Kermit, October 2, 1903

What a heavenly place a sandbox is for two little boys! Archie and Quentin play industriously in it during most of their spare moments when out in the grounds. I often look out of the office windows when I have a score of Senators and Congressmen with me and see them both hard at work arranging caverns or mountains, with runways for their marbles.

—Letter to Kermit, March 11, 1906,
quoted in *A Bully Father: Theodore Roosevelt's Letters to His Children*
by Joan Paterson Kerr

I can do one of two things, I can be President of the United States or I can control Alice. I can't possibly do both.

—Roosevelt's response to novelist Owen Wister, who asked why Roosevelt
couldn't control his daughter's unruly behavior, circa 1901.
Quoted in *The Roosevelts: An American Saga*
by Peter Collier with David Horowitz

Home, wife, and children—they are what really count in life. I have enjoyed many things; the Presidency, my success as a soldier, a writer, a big game hunter and explorer; but all of them put together are not for one moment to be weighed in the balance when compared with the joy I have known with your mother and all of you.

—Letter to Ted, Jr., quoted in *Lion in the White House:
A Life of Theodore Roosevelt* by Aida D. Donald

The children are no longer children now. Most of them are men and women, working out their own fates in the big world; some in our own land, others across the great oceans or where the Southern Cross blazes in the tropic nights. Some of them have children of their own; some are working at one thing, some at another; in cable ships, in business offices, in factories, in newspaper offices, building steel bridges, bossing gravel trains and steam shovels, or laying tracks and superintending freight traffic. They have had their share of accidents and escapes. . . . They have known and they will know joy and sorrow, triumph and temporary defeat. But I believe they are all the better off because of their happy and healthy childhood.

— *An Autobiography,* 1913

The one thing I want to leave my children is an honorable name. It is hard to fail, but it is worse never to have tried to succeed.

— Speech, "The Strenuous Life," Chicago, April 10, 1899

BOOKS, SPORT, AND LIFE'S PLEASURES

I could not name any principle upon which the books have been gathered. Books are almost as individual as friends. There is no earthly use in laying down general laws about them. . . . Personally the books by which I have profited infinitely more than by any others have been those in which profit was a by-product of the pleasure; that is, I read them because I enjoyed them, because I liked reading them, and the profit came in as part of the enjoyment.

—*An Autobiography*, 1913

Fortunately I had enough good sense, or obstinacy, or something, to retain a subconscious belief that inasmuch as books were meant to be read, good books ought to be interesting, and the best books capable in addition of giving one a lift upward in some direction.

—Letter to Sir George Otto Trevelyan, January 23, 1904

It always interests me about Dickens to think how much first-class work he did and how almost all of it was mixed up with every kind of cheap, second-rate matter. I am very fond of him. There are innumerable characters that he has created which symbolize vices, virtues, follies, and the like almost as well as the characters in Bunyan; and therefore I think the wise thing to do is simply to skip the bosh and twaddle and vulgarity and untruth, and get the benefit out of the rest. Of course one fundamental difference between Thackeray and Dickens is that Thackeray was a gentleman and Dickens was not. But a man might do some mighty good work and not be a gentleman in any sense.

—Letter to his son Kermit, February 23, 1908

Normally I only care for a novel if the ending is good. I quite agree with you that if the hero has to die he ought to die worthily and nobly, so that our sorrow at the tragedy shall be tempered with the joy and pride one always feels when a man does his duty well and bravely.

—Letter to his son Kermit, referring to *Nicholas Nickleby*
by Charles Dickens, November 19, 1905

I find reading a great comfort. People often say to me that they do not see how I find time for it, to which I answer them (much more truthfully than they believe) that to me it is a dissipation, which I have sometimes to try to avoid, instead of an irksome duty. Of course I have been so busy for the last ten years, so absorbed in political work, that I have simply given up reading any book that I do not find interesting. But there are a great many books which ordinarily pass for "dry" which to me do possess much interest—notably history and anthropology; and these give me ease and relaxation that I can get in no other way, not even on horseback!

—Letter to George Otto Trevelyan, May 28, 1904

Many learned people seem to feel that the quality of readableness in a book is one which warrants suspicion. Indeed, not a few learned people seem to feel that the fact that a book is interesting is proof that it is shallow.

—Address, "History as Literature," American Historical Association,
Boston, December 27, 1912

My maternal grandfather's house was on the line of Sherman's march to the sea, and pretty much everything in it that was portable was taken by the boys in blue, including most of the books in the library. When I was President the facts about my ancestry were published and a former soldier in Sherman's army sent me back one of the books with my grandfather's name in it. It was a little copy of the poems of "Mr. Gray"—an eighteenth-century edition printed in Glasgow.

—*An Autobiography,* 1913

There should be a national gallery of art established in the capital city of this country. This is important not merely to the artistic but to the material welfare of the country; and the people are to be congratulated on the fact that the movement to establish such a gallery is taking definite form under the guidance of the Smithsonian Institution. So far from there being a tariff on works of art brought into the country, their importation should be encouraged in every way. There have been no sufficient collections of objects of art by the government, and what collections have been acquired are scattered and are generally placed in unsuitable and imperfectly lighted galleries.

—Annual Message to Congress, December 3, 1907

Let us profit by the scholarship, art, and literature of every other country and every other time; let us adapt to our own use whatever is of value in any other language, in any other literature, in any other art; but let us keep steadily in mind that in every field of endeavor the work best worth doing for Americans must in some degree express the distinctive characteristics of our own national soul.

—Address before the American Academy and National Institute
of Arts and Letters, New York City, November 16, 1916

A man whose business is sedentary should get some kind of exercise if he wishes to keep himself in as good physical trim as his brethren who do manual labor.

—*An Autobiography,* 1913

Play should never be allowed to interfere with work; and a life devoted merely to play is, of all forms of existence, the most dismal.

—*An Autobiography,* 1913

Of course what we have a right to expect of the American boy is that he shall turn out to be a good American man. Now, the chances are strong that he won't be much of a man unless he is a good deal of a boy. He must not be a coward or a weakling, a bully, a shirk, or a prig. He must work hard and play hard. He must be clean-minded and clean-lived, and able to hold his own under all circumstances and against all comers. It is only on these conditions that he will grow into the kind of American man of whom America can be really proud.

—"The American Boy," *St. Nicholas,* May 1900

I regard boxing, whether professional or amateur, as a first-class sport, and I do not regard it as brutalizing. Of course matches can be conducted under conditions that make them brutalizing. But this is true of football games and of most other rough and vigorous sports.

—*An Autobiography,* 1913

I do not believe there ever was any life more attractive to a vigorous young fellow than life on a cattle ranch in those days. It was a fine, healthy life, too; it taught a man self-reliance, hardihood, and the value of instant decision—in short, the virtues that ought to come from life in the open country.

—*An Autobiography*, 1913

The most thrilling moments of an American hunter's life are those in which, with every sense on the alert, and with nerves strung to the highest point, he is following alone into the heart of its forest fastness the fresh and bloody footprints of an angered grizzly; and no other triumph of American hunting can compare with the victory to be thus gained.

—The Wilderness Hunter, 1893, quoted in *Theodore Roosevelt: An American Mind* edited by Mario R. DiNunzio

I have shot only five kinds of animals which can fairly be called dangerous game—that is, the lion, elephant, rhinoceros, and buffalo in Africa, and the big grizzly bear a quarter of a century ago in the Rockies. . . . As it happened, however, the only narrow escape I personally ever had was from a grizzly, and in Africa the animal killed closest to me was a charging rhinoceros. . . . Another bull elephant, also unwounded, which charged, nearly got me. . . . People have asked me how I felt on this occasion. My answer has always been that I suppose I felt as most men of like experience feel on such occasions. At such a moment a hunter is so very busy that he has no time to get frightened. He wants to get in his cartridges and try another shot.

—*An Autobiography*, 1913

We worked under the scorching midsummer sun when the wide plains shimmered and wavered in the heat; and we knew the freezing misery of riding night guard round the cattle in the late fall round-up. In the soft springtime the stars were glorious in our eyes each night before we fell asleep; and in the winter we rode through blinding blizzards when the driven snow-dust burnt our faces. . . . We knew toil and hardship and hunger and thirst; and we saw men die violent deaths as they worked among the horses and cattle or fought evil feuds with one another; but we felt the beat of hardy life in our veins, and ours was the glory of work and the joy of living.

—*An Autobiography*, 1913

While my interest in natural history has added very little to my sum of achievement, it has added immeasurably to my sum of enjoyment of life.

"My Life as a Naturalist," *The American Museum Journal*, May 1918

I have already lived and enjoyed as much life as any nine other men I have known.

—Quoted in "Roosevelt, the Greatest Outdoor Man" by Arthur K. Willyoung in *Outing*, September 1919

THE NATURAL WORLD AND CONSERVATION

While still a small boy I began to take an interest in natural history. I remember distinctly the first day that I started on my career as zoologist. I was walking up Broadway, and as I passed the market to which I used sometimes to be sent before breakfast to get strawberries I suddenly saw a dead seal laid out on a slab of wood. That seal filled me with every possible feeling of romance and adventure. I asked where it was killed, and was informed in the harbor. I had already begun to read some of Mayne Reid's books and other boys' books of adventure, and I felt that this seal brought all these adventures in realistic fashion before me. As long as that seal remained there I haunted the neighborhood of the market day after day.

—*An Autobiography*, 1913

The romance of my life began here.

—About his time in the Badlands of the Dakota Territory

There can be nothing in the world more beautiful than the Yosemite, the groves of giant sequoias and redwoods, the Canyon of the Colorado, the Canyon of the Yellowstone, the Three Tetons; and our people should see to it that they are preserved for their children and their children's children forever, with their majestic beauty all unmarred.

—*Outdoor Pastimes of the American Hunter*, 1905

We love all the seasons: the snows and bare woods of winter; the rush of growing things and the blossom spray of spring; the yellow grain, the ripening fruits and tasseled corn, and the deep, leafy shades that are heralded by "the green dance of summer"; and the sharp fall winds that tear the brilliant banners with which the trees greet the dying year.

"Outdoors and Indoors," The Outlook, 1913

The birds have come back. Not only song-sparrows and robins, but a winter wren, purple finches and tufted titmice are singing in the garden; and the other morning early Mother and I were waked up by the loud singing of a cardinal bird in the magnolia tree just outside our windows.

—Letter to Kermit, March 20, 1905, quoted in *A Bully Father: Theodore Roosevelt's Letters to His Children* edited by Joan Paterson Kerr

We of an older generation can get along with what we have, though with growing hardship; but in your full manhood and womanhood you will want what nature once so bountifully supplied and man so thoughtlessly destroyed; and because of that want you will reproach us, not for what we have used, but for what we have wasted.

—A Message to the School-Children of the United States, April 15, 1907

If the present rate of forest destruction is allowed to continue, with nothing to offset it, a timber famine in the future is inevitable. Fire, wasteful and destructive forms of lumbering, and the legitimate use, taken together, are destroying our forest resources far more rapidly than they are being replaced. It is difficult to imagine what such a timber famine would mean to our resources.

—Address to the Forest Congress, Washington, D.C., January 5, 1905

Optimism is a good characteristic, but if carried to an excess it becomes foolishness. We are prone to speak of the resources of this country as inexhaustible; this is not so.

—Annual Message to Congress, December 3, 1907

Of all the questions which can come before this nation, short of the actual preservation of its existence in a great war, there is none which compares in importance with the great central task of leaving this land even a better land for our descendants than it is for us, and training them . . . to inhabit the land and pass it on. Conservation is a great moral issue, for it involves the patriotic duty of insuring the safety and continuation of the nation.

—Speech, "New Nationalism," Osawatomie, Kansas, August 31, 1910

More and more, as it becomes necessary to preserve the game, let us hope that the camera will largely supplant the rifle.

—Roosevelt's preface to *Camera Shots at Big Game* by A. G. Wallihan, 1901

To waste, to destroy, our natural resources, to skin and exhaust the land instead of using it so as to increase its usefulness, will result in undermining in the days of our children the very prosperity which we ought by right to hand down to them amplified and developed.

—Annual Message to Congress, December 3, 1907

EDUCATION AND KNOWLEDGE

All the resources we need are in the mind.

—Attributed

Viewed from any angle, ignorance is the costliest crop that can be raised in any part of this Union.

—Speech, "The Education of the Negro,"
Tuskegee Institute, Tuskegee, Alabama, October 24, 1905

I had no idea how beautiful the world was until I got those spectacles. I had been a clumsy and awkward little boy, and while much of my clumsiness and awkwardness was doubtless due to general character-istics, a good deal of it was due to the fact that I could not see and yet was wholly ignorant that I was not seeing. The recollection of this experience gives me a keen sympathy with those who are trying in our public schools and elsewhere to remove the physical causes of deficiency in children, who are often unjustly blamed for being obsti-nate or unambitious, or mentally stupid.

—An Autobiography, 1913

School is an invaluable adjunct to the home, but it is a wretched substitute for it.

—Commencement Address, Michigan Agricultural College,
East Lansing, Michigan, May 31, 1907

I am a part of everything that I have read.

—Remarked in 1906

I thoroughly enjoyed Harvard and I am sure it did me good, but only in the general effect, for there was very little in my actual studies which helped me in after life.

—*An Autobiography*, 1913

From the standpoint of the nation, and from the broader standpoint of mankind, scholarship is of worth chiefly when it is productive, when the scholar not merely receives or acquires, but gives.

—"Productive Scholarship," *The Outlook*, January 13, 1912

There is not in all America a more dangerous trait than the deification of mere smartness unaccompanied by any sense of moral responsibility.

—Speech, Abilene, Kansas, May 2, 1903

The educated man is entitled to no special privilege, save the inestimable privilege of trying to show that his education enables him to take the lead in striving to guide his fellows aright.

—Address at the University of Pennsylvania, Philadelphia, February 22, 1905

To educate a person in mind and not in morals is to educate a menace to society.

—Quoted in "A Textbook of Virtues," *The New York Times*, January 8, 1995

THE BULLY PULPIT

I suppose my critics will call that preaching, but I have got such a bully pulpit!

—Comment to George Haven Putnam, and recalled by Putnam at Roosevelt's eulogy at the Century Club, New York City, 1919

I preach to you, then, my countrymen, that our country calls not for the life of ease but for the life of strenuous endeavor. The twentieth century looms before us big with the fate of many nations. If we stand idly by, if we seek merely swollen, slothful ease and ignoble peace, if we shrink from the hard contests where men must win at hazard of their lives and at the risk of all they hold dear, then the bolder and stronger peoples will pass us by, and will win for themselves the domination of the world. Let us therefore boldly face the life of strife, resolute to do our duty well and manfully; resolute to uphold righteousness by deed and by word; resolute to be both honest and brave, to serve high ideals, yet to use practical methods. Above all, let us shrink from no strife, moral or physical, within or without the nation, provided we are certain that the strife is justified, for it is only through strife, through hard and dangerous endeavor, that we shall ultimately win the goal of true national greatness.

—Speech, "The Strenuous Life," Chicago, April 10, 1899

The leader holds his position purely because he is able to appeal to the conscience and to the reason of those who support him, and the boss holds his position because he appeals to fear of punishment and hope of reward. The leader works in the open, and the boss is covert. The leader leads, and the boss drives.

—Speech, Binghamton, New York, October 24, 1910

Words with me are instruments. I wish to impress upon the people to whom I talk the fact that I am sincere, that I mean exactly what I say, and that I stand for things that are elemental in civilization.

So it is with the orator. It is highly desirable that a leader of opinion in democracy should be able to state his views clearly and convincingly. But all that the oratory can do of value to the community is enable the man thus to explain himself; if it enables the orator to put false values on things, it merely makes him power for mischief. . . . Indeed, it is a sign of marked political weakness in any commonwealth if the people tend to be carried away by mere oratory, if they tend to value words in and for themselves, as divorced from the deeds for which they are supposed to stand. The phrase-maker, the phrase-monger, the ready talker, however great his power, whose speech does not make for courage, sobriety, and right understanding, is simply a noxious element in the body politic, and it speaks ill for the public if he has influence over them. To admire the gift of oratory without regard to the moral quality behind the gift is to do wrong to the republic.

—Address at the Sorbonne, "Citizenship in a Republic," Paris, April 23, 1910

I have a perfect horror of words that are not backed up by deeds.

—Speech, Oyster Bay, New York, July 7, 1915

Friends, I shall ask you to be as quiet as possible. I don't know whether you fully understand that I have just been shot, but it takes more than that to kill a Bull Moose. But fortunately I had my manuscript, so you see I was going to make a long speech, and there is a bullet—there is where the bullet went through—and it probably saved me from it going into my heart. The bullet is in me now, so that I cannot make a very long speech, but I will try my best. And now, friends, I want to take advantage of this incident to say a word of solemn warning to my fellow countrymen. First of all, I want to say this about myself: I have altogether too important things to think of to feel any concern over my own death; and now I cannot speak to you insincerely within five minutes of being shot. I am telling you the literal truth when I say that my concern is for many other things. It is not in the least for my own life. I want you to understand that I am ahead of the game, anyway. No man has had a happier life than I have led; a happier life in every way. I have been able to do certain things that I greatly wished to do, and I am interested in doing other things. I can tell you with absolute truthfulness that I am very much uninterested in whether I am shot or not. . . . I am in this cause with my whole heart and soul. I believe that the Progressive movement is making life a little easier for all our people; a movement to try to take the burdens off the men and especially the women and children of this country. I am absorbed in the success of that movement.

—Speech, Milwaukee, October 14, 1912, given immediately after Roosevelt was shot by a would-be assassin. The bullet, having gone through his eyeglass case and the double-folded pages of his fifty-page speech, struck Roosevelt in the rib, nearly missing his right lung.

When we come to dealing with our social and industrial needs, remedies, rights and wrongs, a ton of oratory is not worth an ounce of hard-headed, kindly common sense.

—Speech at Labor Day Picnic, Chicago, September 3, 1900

We can do a great deal when we undertake, soberly, to do the possible. When we undertake the impossible, we too often fail to do anything at all.

—Speech in Chicago, September 3, 1900

It is not the critic who counts; not the man who points out how the strong man stumbles or where the doer of deeds could have done better. The credit belongs to the man who is actually in the arena, whose face is marred by dust and sweat and blood, who strives valiantly, who errs and comes up short again and again, because there is no effort without error or shortcoming, but who knows the great enthusiasms, the great devotions, who spends himself for a worthy cause; who, at the best, knows, in the end, the triumph of high achievement, and who, at the worst, if he fails, at least he fails while daring greatly, so that his place shall never be with those cold and timid souls who knew neither victory nor defeat.

—Address at the Sorbonne, "Citizenship in a Republic," Paris, April 23, 1910

WIT AND WISDOM

There are two things that I want you to make up your minds to: first, that you are going to have a good time as long as you live—I have no use for the sour-faced man—and next, that you are going to do something worth while, that you are going to work hard and do the things you set out to do.

—Address to schoolchildren, Oyster Bay, New York, December 1898

Get action, do things; be sane; don't fritter away your time; create, act, take a place wherever you are and be somebody: get action.

—Quoted in *The American Political Tradition: And the Men Who Made It*
by Richard Hofstadter

There is a homely adage which runs: "Speak softly and carry a big stick; you will go far."

—Frequent remark of Roosevelt's in speeches and in print

Nine-tenths of wisdom is being wise in time.

—Speech, Lincoln, Nebraska, June 14, 1917

Life brings sorrows and joys alike. It is what a man does with them— not what they do to him—that is the true test of his mettle.

—Quoted in *The Courage and Character of Theodore Roosevelt*
by George Grant

I believe in realizable ideals and in realizing them, in preaching what can be practiced and then in practicing it.

—*An Autobiography*, 1913

Cowardice is the unpardonable sin.

—Quoted in *The American Experience*, PBS, aired in 1996

In a crisis, the man worth his salt is the man who meets the needs of the situation in whatever way is necessary.

—*An Autobiography*, 1913

It is impossible to win the great prizes of life without running risks, and the greatest of all prizes are those connected with the home. No father and mother can hope to escape sorrow and anxiety, and there are dreadful moments when death comes very near those we love, even if for the time being it passes by. But life is a great adventure, and the worst of all fears is the fear of living.

—*An Autobiography*, 1913

Black care rarely sits beside the rider whose pace is fast enough.

—Quoted in *The Presidential Character: Predicting Performance in the White House* by James David Barber

I have never in my life envied a human being who led an easy life; I have envied a great many people who led difficult lives and led them well.

—Speech in Des Moines, Iowa, November 4, 1910

Do what you can, with what you have, where you are.

—A favorite saying of Roosevelt's

Far and away the best prize that life offers is the chance to work hard at work worth doing.

—Labor Day Address, Syracuse, New York, September 7, 1903

There can be no falser standard [of success] than that set by the deification of material well-being in and for itself.

—Address at the Sorbonne, "Citizenship in a Republic," Paris, April 23, 1910

Bodily vigor is good, and vigor of intellect is even better, but far above is character.

—"Character and Success," *The Outlook*, March 31, 1900

You can be sure that these younger people will follow your example and not your precept. It is no use to preach to them if you do not act decently yourself.

—Speech to Holy Name Society, Oyster Bay, New York, August 16, 1903

I never keep boys waiting. It's a hard trial for a boy to wait.

—Quoted in *The Life and Meaning of Theodore Roosevelt* by Eugene Thwing

Unrestricted individualism spells ruin to the individual himself. But so does the elimination of individualism, whether by law or custom.

—*An Autobiography*, 1913

A man who never has gone to school may steal from a freight car, but if he has a university education, he may steal from the whole railroad.

—Attributed

There is no greater duty than to war on the corrupt and unprincipled boss, and on the corrupt and unprincipled business man; and for the matter of that, the corrupt and unprincipled labor leader also, and on the corrupt and unprincipled editor, and on any one else who is corrupt and unprincipled.

—*An Autobiography*, 1913

By George, I don't believe I ever do talk with a man five minutes without liking him very much, unless I disliked him very much.

—Quoted in *Theodore Roosevelt: Icon of the American Century* by James G. Barber

To borrow a simile from the football field, we believe that men must play fair, but that there must be no shirking, and that the success can only come to the player who hits the line hard.

—Remarks at Sagamore Hill, Oyster Bay, New York, October 1897

Courage, hard work, self-mastery, and intelligent effort are all essential to successful life.

—*America and the World War*, 1915

Be practical as well as generous in your ideals. Keep your eyes on the stars, but remember to keep your feet on the ground. Be truthful; a lie implies fear, vanity, or malevolence; be frank; furtiveness and insincerity are faults incompatible with true manliness. Be honest, and remember that honesty counts for nothing unless back of it lie courage and efficiency.

—Speech, Groton School, Groton, Massachusetts, May 24, 1904

THEODORE ROOSEVELT: THE MAN AND HIS LEGACY

I am still looking forward, not back. I do not know any man who has had as happy a fifty years as I have had. I have had about as good a run for my money as any human being possibly could have; and whatever happens now I am ahead of the game.

—Letter to Frederic Remington, October 28, 1908

I am not in the least a hero, my dear fellow. I am a perfectly common-place man and I know it; I am just a decent American citizen who tries to stand for what is decent in his own country and in other countries and who owes very much to you and to certain men like you who are not fellow countrymen of his.

—Letter to George Otto Trevelyan, May 29, 1915

I don't mind having to die. I've had my good time . . . and I don't mind having to pay for it. But to think that those swine will say that I'm out of the game. . . .

—Remarked to a friend about his political enemies while bed-ridden in great pain a year before his death, February 1918. Quoted in *Power and Responsibility: The Life and Times of Theodore Roosevelt* by William Henry Harbaugh

As he went on a quest for vigor and a strenuous life, he practiced what one of his friends called "his policy of forcing the spirit to ignore the weakness of the flesh." He urged others to learn from his experience that "man does in fact become fearless by sheer dint of practicing fearlessness."

—*Theodore Roosevelt: A Strenuous Life* by Kathleen Dalton

He was viewed as an oddity by his cowhands, but he gradually won respect by his hard work, forthrightness, and courage. One incident that became locally famous occurred when he went into the tiny town of Mingusville. . . . Overtaken by darkness, he went to the town's ramshackle hotel to get out of the cold. Going into the bar for a cup of coffee, he saw a dangerous situation—a man drunkenly waving a pair of revolvers and talking with "strident profanity" while a frightened group of onlookers cowered. . . .

"Four Eyes is going to treat," the man said when he saw TR. Roosevelt joined in the laugh and sat down at a table, ignoring the threat. The drunk came over and stood above him, a gun in each hand, using foul language as he again commanded him to buy drinks. "Well, if I've got to, I've got to," Roosevelt shrugged. Standing up quickly, he suddenly struck the man in the face with both fists. Both guns discharged as the drunk went down, unconscious, but no one was hit. TR disarmed him and the others dragged him out to a shed to sleep it off until morning when he was put aboard the first train out of town.

—*The Roosevelts: An American Saga* by Peter Collier with David Horowitz

He settled the great anthracite coal strike of 1902 by entering the mediation as no President had done before. He initiated the first successful antitrust suit against a corporate monopoly, the giant Northern Securities Company (and when his father's old friend J.P. Morgan came to Washington to demand an explanation, such action served only to harden his resolve). He "took the Isthmus" and built the Panama Canal, and served as a peacemaker in the Russo-Japanese War, for which he received the Nobel Peace Prize.

—*Mornings on Horseback* by David McCullough

He put new morale into the Force. . . . No man was afraid to do his duty while Roosevelt was commissioner, because he knew that the commissioner was behind him. The crooks were afraid of the cops—and the cops were not afraid of the crooks. All the decent, manly fellows on the Force loved this strenuous master who led them. He was human. You could talk to him. . . . He had an open door for any member of the Force. Every man who really tried to do right or, having gone crooked, reformed and showed he was trying to do right, always received a fair chance. He detested cowardice and shirking . . . but he always stuck to the man who proved he was doing or trying to do his job. . . . I guess that nine-tenths of the men that's ever come in contact with Theodore Roosevelt are better and squarer men because of it.

> —A captain recalls Roosevelt as New York City Police Commissioner, quoted in *Theodore Roosevelt: The Great Adventure and the Rise of Modern America* by Albert Marrin

Try as he might to become a westerner, TR could never shed his eastern persona. His manner of speaking often betrayed him. On one occasion he told a fellow cowhand, "Hasten forward quickly there!" The man's comrades reeled with laughter, which in turn echoed in barrooms throughout the territory.

> —*Theodore Roosevelt: Icon of the American Century* by James G. Barber

Thee is so able and no mistake—shrewd and clever, by no means behind the age. What I have often smiled at in the Old Boy are I am now sure some of his best points—a practical carrying out in action of what I, for example, am convinced of in theory but fail to put into practice.

> —Elliott Roosevelt about his brother Theodore, quoted in *The Roosevelts: An American Saga* by Peter Collier with David Horowitz

Roosevelt's courtesy is not extended only to the well-born. The President of the United States leaps automatically from his chair when a woman enters the room, even if she is the governess of his children. Introduced to a party of people who pointedly ignore their own chauffeur, he protests: "I have not met this gentleman." He has never been able to get used to the fact that White House stewards serve him ahead of the ladies at his table, but accepts it as necessary protocol.

—*The Rise of Theodore Roosevelt* by Edmund Morris

[He is] the most perfectly equipped and most efficient politician thus far seen in the Presidency.

—Ex-President Grover Cleveland's assessment of Theodore Roosevelt, quoted in *The Rise of Theodore Roosevelt* by Edmund Morris

---

One of his friends, the English diplomat Cecil Spring Rice, once said, "The thing you have to remember about the President is he's about six." Woodrow Wilson called him a "great big boy." He went off later in life, after leaving the White House, on a very dangerous, very risky adventure in South America, and when they asked him why he was doing it at his age, he said, "It's my last chance to be a boy again."

—David McCullough, *The American Experience*, PBS, aired in 1996

I could not believe it this morning when I heard the news of his death. He seemed to be a great elemental force, like Niagara or the Hudson River.

—John Quinn, friend of Roosevelt, quoted in *A Strenuous Life* by Kathleen Dalton

Mrs. Roosevelt has let it be known that she considers him one of her own brood, to be disciplined accordingly when necessary. Between conferences he loves to sneak upstairs to the attic; headquarters for Quentin's "White House Gang," and thunder up and down in pursuit of squealing boys. These romps leave him so disheveled he has to change his shirt before returning to his duties.

— *The Rise of Theodore Roosevelt* by Edmund Morris

He is, fortunately, a superb talker, with a gift for le mot juste that stings and sizzles. Although he hardly ever swears—his intolerance of bad language verges on the prissy—he can pack such venom into a word like "swine" that it has the force of an obscenity. . . . Roosevelt has a particular gift for humorous invective. Old-timers still talk about the New York Supreme Court justice he pilloried as "an amiable old fuzzy-wuzzy with sweetbread brains." Critics of the Administration's Panama policy are "a small bunch of shrill eunuchs"; demonstrators against bloodsports are "logical vegetarians of the flabbiest Hindoo type." President Castro of Venezuela is "an unspeakably villainous little monkey."

— *The Rise of Theodore Roosevelt* by Edmund Morris

Something was going on every minute of the day. The house was full of people. Conferences went on all day. The telephone never stopped ringing. In the evenings my father-in-law received the newspapermen. At first I thought everyone would be tired when the day was over and would go to bed early, but I soon found out that nothing of the kind could be expected. The Roosevelt family enjoyed life too much to waste time sleeping. Every night they stayed downstairs until nearly midnight; then, talking at the top of their voices, they trooped up the wide uncarpeted stairs and went to their rooms. For a brief moment all was still, but just as I was going off to sleep for the second time they remembered things they have forgotten to tell one another and ran shouting through the halls. I tried going to bed with cotton in my ears, but it never did any good.

—Eleanor Alexander Roosevelt, Ted's wife, about life at Sagamore Hill in the summer of 1912, quoted in *Roosevelt the Explorer* by H. Paul Jeffers

The president's put-downs became legendary. Once Roosevelt lambasted a British diplomat, saying he had "a brain of about eight-guinea pig-power." Of a rival politician Roosevelt said, "Every time he opens his mouth, he subtracts from the sum total of human wisdom." When Oliver Wendell Holmes Jr., a respected Supreme Court justice, disagreed with him, Roosevelt snapped: "I could carve out of a banana a judge with more backbone than that."

—*The Great Adventure: Theodore Roosevelt and the Rise of Modern America* by Albert Marrin

"[A] filthy little atheist."

—On Thomas Paine, *The Dictionary of American Biography* edited by Dumas Malone

His knowledge stretched from babies to the post-Alexandrian kingdoms and, what was more, he could always lay his hands on it. It made little difference in what channels the conversation turned. Sooner or later he was able to produce information which often startled students of the theme under discussion.

—Ted Roosevelt about his father, quoted in *Roosevelt the Explorer* by H. Paul Jeffers

The tale is that while Roosevelt was hunting with a party in Mississippi in 1902, with no success in bagging a much-wanted bear, his friends found a cub and tied it to a tree, ready for shooting. Roosevelt refused the offer as unsporting and let the bear go, with the result that fake baby bears were named Teddy and became an instant and favorite child's toy for generations.

—*Lion in the White House: A Life of Theodore Roosevelt* by Aida D. Donald

Roosevelt was a many-sided man and every side was like an electric battery. Such versatility, such vitality, such thoroughness, such copiousness, have rarely been united in one man. He was not only a full man, he was also a ready man and an exact man. He could bring all his vast resources of power and knowledge to bear upon a given subject instantly.

—*Natural History Journal of the American Museum*,
John Burroughs, January 1919

The real builder of the Panama Canal was Theodore Roosevelt.

—George Washington Goethals, the Panama Canal's chief engineer,
quoted in *Great Moments in History* by David McCullough

Never before in my life has it been so hard for me to accept the death of any man as it has been for me to accept the death of Theodore Roosevelt. A pall seems to settle upon the very sky. The world is bleaker and colder for his absence from it. We shall not look upon his like again.

—Naturalist John Burroughs, quoted in *The River of Doubt:
Theodore Roosevelt's Darkest Journey* by Candice Millard

Ironically, he who had worried that he might never live up to his father's name loomed so large in his own time that he obliterated his father's name. Only one Theodore Roosevelt was to be remembered, once his father's generation had passed from the scene.

—*Mornings on Horseback* by David McCullough

With the passing of Theodore Roosevelt passes the world's greatest protagonist of lofty ideals and principles. Take him all in all he was a man, generous, impulsive, fearless, loving the public eye, but intent on achieving the public good. . . . We mourn with the rest of the world as is fitting, but there is too in our sorrow a quality peculiar and apart. We have lost a friend. That he was our friend proves the justice of our cause, for Roosevelt never championed a cause which was not in essence right.

—NAACP eulogy upon Roosevelt's death, quoted in *Theodore Roosevelt: A Strenuous Life* by Kathleen Dalton

Something like a superman in the political sphere has passed away. He saw the nation steadily and he saw it whole. Where other politicians dealt with individuals, Mr. Roosevelt reached out for vast groups. . . . He boldly thrust out his hand and captured the hearts and the suffrages of a whole race, an entire church, a block of states. Never have we had a politician who, with such an appearance of effortless ease, drew after him great masses and moulded them to his will.

—*The New York Evening Post,* upon Roosevelt's death, quoted in *Colonel Roosevelt* by Edmund Morris

Father always wanted to be the corpse at every funeral, the bride at every wedding and the baby at every christening.

—Alice Roosevelt, quoted in *A Bully Father: Theodore Roosevelt's Letters to His Children* edited by Joan Paterson Kerr

No president has acted as vigorously to protect the national resources as Roosevelt. Before Roosevelt presidents really weren't concerned with . . . our national resources. He was really the greatest conservationist president in our history and he faced down special interests to save over 230 million acres of wilderness for us and our descendants. Well, today we face similar problems. What should the government's role be in protecting our environment? For TR, there wasn't a question there. He went out and acted in the interest of the environment.

—David Gruben, *The American Experience*, PBS, aired in 1996

The future we cannot see; nor what the next imperious task; nor who its strong executant. But for this generation the task is clear: you who gird yourselves for this great fight in the never-ending warfare for the good of mankind, we stand at Armageddon and we battle for the Lord.

—Speech, Progressive Party Convention, Chicago, August 6, 1912

The most striking figure in American life.

—Thomas Edison, about Roosevelt, quoted in *Mornings on Horseback* by David McCullough

Let us stand valiantly for what is decent and right; let us strike hard, and take with unshaken front whatever comes, whether it be good or ill. Then the fates must decide what the outcome will be.

—Quoted in *Presidential Government*, Volume 2, by James MacGregor Burns

I met in him a man of such extraordinary power that to find a second at the same time on this globe would have been an impossibility; a man whom to associate with was a liberal education, and who could be in every way likened to radium, for warmth, force and light emanated from him and no spending of it could ever diminish his store. A man of immense interests, there was nothing in which he did not feel that there was something worthy of study; people of today, people of yesterday, animals, minerals, stones, stars, the past, the future—everything was of interest for him. He studied each thing, knew something about every subject.

—Address by Jean J. Jusserand, to the Rocky Mountain Club, on the anniversary of Roosevelt's death, October 27, 1919

CHRONOLOGY

October 27, 1858 — Theodore Roosevelt is born at 28 East 20th Street, New York City. He is the son of Theodore Roosevelt, Sr., and Martha (Mittie) Bulloch Roosevelt. The couple's first child, Anna, was born in 1855. The household also includes maternal aunt Anna Bulloch and grandmother Martha Stewart Elliott Bulloch.

1860 — Brother Elliott is born.

1861 — Theodore Roosevelt, Sr., does not enlist in the Union Army because of his wife's objections—she is Southern, a supporter of the Confederacy, and has two brothers fighting for the South. He works tirelessly to help establish an Allotment Commission which ultimately results in millions of dollars of the soldiers' pay going home to their families. He is away from home for long periods of time during the first two years of the war, lobbying the government and visiting army camps. Another child, Corinne, is born.

1862 — Roosevelt begins to experience acute nighttime asthma attacks.

1865 — Roosevelt watches Abraham Lincoln's funeral procession on April 25, 1865, from his grandfather's house located at Broadway and 14th Street.

1876 — After a childhood of being home-schooled along with his siblings and family friend Edith Kermit Carow by his aunt Anna Bulloch, and having developed a love of reading and natural history, Roosevelt enters Harvard College.

1878 — Theodore Roosevelt, Sr., dies of cancer of the bowel on February 9. Roosevelt is inconsolable. He spends time alone hunting and rowing to escape his grief. Back at Harvard for his junior year, Roosevelt meets Alice Hathaway Lee, a seventeen-year-old beauty and cousin of a friend. He is immediately smitten with her.

1880 — Roosevelt finally persuades Alice Lee to marry him. They are engaged on January 25. Roosevelt graduates from Harvard, *magna cum laude*, in June and marries Alice Lee on October 27, in Brookline, Massachusetts. The couple moves to the Roosevelt family home on West 57th Street and Roosevelt enters Columbia law school.

1881 — Roosevelt is elected to New York State Assembly as a Republican from the 21st District.

1882 — Roosevelt publishes his first book, *The Naval War of 1812*. He ends his legal studies, and the couple move to a house at 55 West 45th Street.

1883 — Elected minority leader of New York State Assembly. He works with Democrat and New York State Governor Grover Cleveland to pass a civil service reform bill; and the bill Roosevelt sponsored prohibiting the home manufacture of cigars after touring through New York City tenements is made into law. Roosevelt travels to the Badlands, Dakota Territory, and invests in two cattle ranches. He is re-elected to the Assembly in November.

1884 — On February 12, the couple's child, Alice Lee Roosevelt, is born. Roosevelt is in Albany at the time and is elated at the news. He soon receives an urgent telegram to get home immediately. He arrives to find his wife delirious and near death from the previously undiagnosed Bright's disease, and his mother in the last stages of typhoid fever. They both die on February 14. Roosevelt writes in his diary, "The light has gone out of my life." In June, Roosevelt is the delegate to the Republican National Convention in Chicago. In July, he travels to the Dakota Badlands to become a cattle rancher. He gives his infant daughter, Alice, to his sister Anna to raise in his absence. He comes back in December to visit with Alice and Anna.

1885 — He travels back to the Badlands for the spring roundup. The house in Oyster Bay, now named "Sagamore Hill," on land that he'd purchased before Alice died, was completed. He publishes *Hunting Trips of a Ranchman* in July. While visiting his sister Anna in September, he encounters Edith Carow, his childhood friend and a lifelong friend of his sister. By mid-November, they become secretly engaged.

1886 — Roosevelt is defeated in his mayoral bid in New York City in November. In December, he sails to England and marries Edith Kermit Carow in London.

1887 —After their honeymoon, the couple moves to Sagamore Hill and takes young Alice to live with them, devastating his sister Anna, who was raising the child. Roosevelt ends his active dealings with the ranches, but returns to hunt. He publishes *Life of Thomas Hart Benton*. The couple's first child, Theodore Jr. is born. The couple has four more children: Kermit (1889); Ethel (1891); Archibald (1894); and Quentin (1897).

1888 — Roosevelt publishes *Gouverneur Morris* and begins work on what will become the multiple-volume *The Winning of the West*. He also publishes *Ranch Life and the Hunting Trail*.

1889–1895 — *The Winning of the West* is published in four volumes from 1889 to 1896. Roosevelt is appointed and serves as one of three Civil Service commissioners by President Benjamin Harrison. He is reappointed by President Grover Cleveland. He publishes *History of the City of New York* in 1891. He attempts but fails to have his brother Elliott declared legally insane after his years of drinking and mental imbalance. He persuades his brother to enter a sanitarium in 1892. In 1893, Roosevelt publishes *The Wilderness Hunter*. In 1894, his brother Elliott dies from a seizure. Roosevelt resigns as Civil Service commissioner in 1895. He is appointed to the New York City Police Commission in April of 1895 and is elected president of the Board of Police Commissioners in May. He spearheads the resignation of the current chief who is reportedly involved with corruption. He begins walking the beat in New York at night to check up on the police officers. He publishes the children's book *Hero Tales from American History*, written with Henry Cabot Lodge.

1897 — On April 6, he is appointed assistant secretary of the navy by President McKinley and resigns as police commissioner. He advocates a program of rapid naval expansion. He publishes *American Ideals*, a book of his essays and speeches.

1898 —The U.S. battleship *Maine* explodes in Havana harbor on February 15. Though the cause of the explosion was not determined, Roosevelt sends orders for the navy to prepare for possible war with Spain. On April 24, Spain declares war on the U.S. over U.S. support of the Cuban independence movement. On April 25, war with Spain is declared by the U.S. Roosevelt resigns his position and is commissioned as lieutenant colonel of the First U.S. Cavalry Volunteer Regiment. The media deems the regiment as Roosevelt's "Rough Riders." Roosevelt is promoted to colonel on June 30, and leads cavalry charges up Kettle Hill and San Juan Hill in the battle for San Juan Heights. An armistice ending the war between the U.S. and Spain is signed on August 12. Roosevelt returns to the U.S. a war hero on August 15 and is elected the governor of New York on November 8.

1900 — Roosevelt publishes *Oliver Cromwell*. As governor, Roosevelt wins passage of landmark legislation to tax the franchises providing public utilities; he went after large corporations and pushed through bills to improve labor conditions, as well as legislation aimed at promoting conservation of the state's natural resources. In an effort to get Roosevelt out of New York politics, a movement begins to nominate Roosevelt as the vice presidential candidate. In June, he receives the party's nomination, and in November, McKinley and Roosevelt win the election. During the campaign, Roosevelt publishes *The Strenuous Life*, another collection of his essays and speeches.

1901 — President McKinley is shot by an assassin on September 6. On September 14, McKinley dies and Roosevelt is sworn into office as the 26th president. He invites Booker T. Washington to dinner at the White House on October 16, to the outrage of many Southerners.

1902 — Department of Justice files antitrust suit against Northern Securities Company; more than forty antitrust indictments follow between 1902 and 1909. In May, the first of five national parks is created by Roosevelt. In December, he relies on the Monroe Doctrine to persuade Germany to act on Venezuela's nonpayment of loans from German banks.

1903 — On February 14, the Departments of Commerce and Labor are set up. Later in the month, the Elkins Antirebate Act is signed, ending preferential railroad shipping rates. In March, the first federal bird refuge is set up; fifty more will follow. On November 7, the administration recognizes the Republic of Panama, after it declared independence from Colombia. On November 18, the Panama Canal Treaty is signed between Panama and the U.S., which results in the building of the Panama Canal, which is completed in 1914.

1904 — Roosevelt is nominated and is elected with Charles W. Fairbanks as his Vice President. In December, Roosevelt announces a "Roosevelt Corollary" to the Monroe Doctrine in his annual message to Congress; this enables the U.S. to police Latin America.

1905 — In January, Roosevelt creates the first of four federal game preserves. In February, the U.S. Forest Service is created. During his administration, the federal forest reserves expand from 43,000,000 to about 194,000,000 acres. In August, Roosevelt meets with and mediates between Russian and Japanese diplomats, and helps to end the Russo-Japanese War.

1906 — Roosevelt mediates dispute between France and Germany over Morocco. He signs the Antiquities or National Monuments Act to preserve so-called national monuments; the Hepburn Act, giving the ICC authority over railroad rates; as well as the Pure Food and Drug Act and Meat Inspection Act. In November, he is widely criticized by black leaders after he dishonorably discharges 167 black soldiers accused of mayhem in Texas. No convictions ensue. In December, Roosevelt is awarded the Nobel Peace Prize for his role in ending the Russo-Japanese War. He donates the money to charity.

1907 — Sends a U.S. battle fleet known as the "Great White Fleet" around the world to demonstrate U.S. naval power.

1909 — William Howard Taft, Roosevelt's chosen successor, is inaugurated. Roosevelt leaves for a year-long safari to Africa.

1910 — Delivers "New Nationalism" speech in Kansas detailing his progressive philosophy.

1912 — Roosevelt challenges Taft for Republican presidential nomination in February and in August creates his National Progressive Party to continue his bid for the presidency. On October 14, he is shot by a would-be assassin in Milwaukee but delivers his speech before going to the hospital. In November, Woodrow Wilson is elected president but Roosevelt comes in second in the voting. In December, he is elected president of the American Historical Association.

1914 — Travels with expedition sponsored by the American Museum of Natural History and the Brazilian government, and discovers the 900-mile so-called "River of Doubt."

1916 — Roosevelt declines the Progressive Party's presidential nomination.

1917 — U.S. enters World War I. Roosevelt offers to raise and lead a volunteer division, but Wilson declines his offer. All of Roosevelt's sons serve in France.

1918 — Roosevelt's youngest son, Quentin, is killed in France as a fighter pilot.

1919 — Roosevelt dies in his sleep at Sagamore Hill at the age of 60 from what is believed to be a pulmonary embolism.

Image Credits

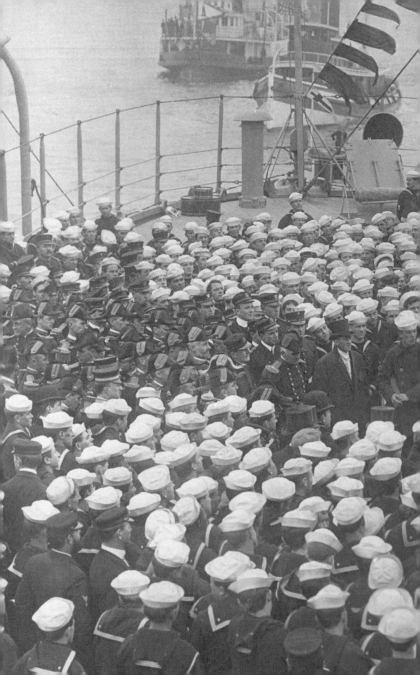